Thinking from A to Z, 3rd Edition

How do politicians win arguments? By not giving a direct answer to a direct question. The **politician's answer** is a form of economy with the truth.

'Mick Jagger and I went to the same primary school; Mick Jagger turned out to be a great success, so I will too.' Why is this a **fallacy**?

Where would you find **gobbledygook**? See **jargon**, **pseudo-profundity** and **smokescreen**.

Being able to spot poor reasoning and diversionary ploys like these will put more clout behind your arguments and sharpen your thinking.

This brilliant book, now in its third edition, will give you the power to tell a good from a bad argument. Using witty and topical examples, Nigel Warburton will enable you to distinguish with confidence between a **red herring** and a **straw man**.

This updated third edition includes new entries on:

principle of charity	**sentimentality**
lawyer's answer	**sunk cost fallacy**
least worst option	**weasel words**
poisoning the well	**'you would say that wouldn't you'**

Nigel Warburton is the author of *Philosophy: The Basics* (4th edition), *Philosophy: The Classics* (3rd edition), *Philosophy: The Essential Study Guide*, *Freedom*, *The Art Question* and *The Basics of Essay Writing*, and is editor of *Philosophy: Basic Readings* (2nd edition).

Y

you too

A variety of the **companions in guilt move**, the equivalent of saying, 'This criticism doesn't just apply to my position; it applies to yours too.' (See also *ad hominem* **move** in the second sense given in that entry.)

'you would say that wouldn't you'

A particular kind of **getting personal** (or *ad hominem* **move**). Those who use this phrase typically do so to undermine the credibility of a speaker by pointing out the **vested interest** or highly motivated nature of their comments. During the *Profumo* trial, Mandy Rice-Davies famously said of the then Lord Astor's denial of an affair with her 'He would say that wouldn't he', drawing attention to his motivation for denial. In that case it was certainly relevant and appropriate to make the remark, and it was devastatingly effective. However, in some other cases drawing attention to the speaker's motives may deflect attention away from any arguments or evidence that the speaker is actually using. These should be assessed independently of a speaker's motives.

For example, someone who is both health-conscious and loves wine might cite scientific evidence to support the idea that drinking moderate amounts of red wine has beneficial effects. This might elicit the response 'you would say that wouldn't you', which would draw attention to the speaker's vested interest in discovering that wine-drinking is compatible with a healthy lifestyle. Yet the speaker's motivation cannot affect the evidence: that stands or falls whether or not the speaker is motivated to cite it. As long as the speaker isn't misrepresenting the evidence (and possible counter-evidence or **alternative explanations** of this apparent health-giving effect), then the charge 'you would say that wouldn't you' does not touch the facts; it only reveals something about why the speaker might be so keen to cite those facts.

The phrase is best used against a speaker who, like Lord Astor, merely asserts a position that they are highly motivated to defend, rather than against those who use argument and evidence to support what they say (which may also be highly motivated). In the latter sort of case, whilst understanding motivation gives us a fuller picture, it should not cloud the issue and prevent us from judging the arguments and evidence as presented.

Z

zig-zagging

Jumping from one topic to another in a discussion as a defence against criticism. This is closely linked with **shifting the goalposts** and with the technique of the **politician's answer**. However, whereas shifting the goalposts involves changing the point of the discussion, and a politician's answer is really just a form of **irrelevance**, zig-zagging involves hopping from one topic to another, typically from one relevant topic to another relevant one. This can be particularly frustrating in discussion because zig-zaggers never rest long enough on one topic for you to present your criticism; by the time you have started to put forward your objections, they are off on a different tack. This can be used as a form of **rhetoric** to avoid facing criticism and thereby make one's position more persuasive; however, it is often simply due to superficiality and not having the intellectual energy to follow any discussion through.

For instance, someone might begin a discussion on the need for longer prison sentences as a deterrent against violent crime by arguing that the expense of such a measure to a government is justified in that it increases security for law-abiding citizens. However, at the point when a critic is about to present empirical evidence that such measures have never actually led to a decrease in violent crime, the first speaker might perform a zig-zag, shifting discussion on to the related topic of the question of whether or not the police should carry firearms. Such zig-zagging makes it almost impossible to engage in serious debate because any criticism is likely to seem irrelevant to the topic currently under discussion.

Thinking
from
A to Z

3rd Edition

If you can't say it clearly, you don't
understand it yourself.
John Searle

- Nigel Warburton

Routledge
Taylor & Francis Group

LONDON AND NEW YORK

First published 1996
by Routledge
2 Park Square, Milton Park,
Abingdon, Oxon OX14 4RN

Simultaneously published in the
USA and Canada
by Routledge
270 Madison Ave, New York,
NY10016

Second edition published 2000

This edition published 2007

*Routledge is an imprint of the
Taylor & Francis Group, an informa
business*

© 1996, 2000, 2007 Nigel Warburton

Typeset in Times and Frutiger
by Florence Production Ltd,
Stoodleigh, Devon
Printed and bound in Great Britain
by TJ International Ltd, Padstow,
Cornwall

*British Library Cataloguing in
Publication Data*
A catalogue record for this book is
available from the British Library.

*Library of Congress Cataloging in
Publication Data*
A catalog record for this book has
been applied for.

ISBN10: 0–415–43371–1

ISBN13: 978–0–415–43371–6

In memory of Matthew (1958–93)

Contents

Acknowledgements

I am grateful for comments that various people have made on parts of this book. In particular I want to thank James Cargile, Simon Christmas, Michael Clark, Shirley Coulson, Jonathan Hourigan, Robin Le Poidevin, Jonathan Lowe, Richard Mascall, Lotte Motz, Alex Orenstein, Tom Stoneham, Anne Thomson, Jennifer Trusted, Jamie Whyte, and several anonymous readers. My wife Anna's many perceptive criticisms made this a much better book than it would otherwise have been.

Nigel Warburton
Website: www.nigelwarburton.com
Weblog: www.nigelwarburton.typepad.com

Introduction

This book is an introduction to critical thinking. It provides some of the basic tools for clear thinking on any issue. The techniques and topics discussed can be applied to any area in which clear thought is required: they have direct applications in most academic disciplines and in any facet of life in which people present reasons and evidence in support of conclusions.

There are four main sorts of entry. First, there are those which deal with common moves in argument such as the **companions in guilt move**. Then there are those which focus on seductive reasoning errors such as the **correlation = cause confusion** and the **Van Gogh fallacy**. There are entries on techniques of persuasion and avoidance, such as the **no hypotheticals move** and the **politician's answer**. And, lastly, there are those which examine psychological factors which can be obstacles to clear thought, such as **wishful thinking**. Not all of the entries fit neatly into these categories, but most of them do. Each entry contains a short account of a topic, usually followed by examples. The examples are partly there to help you see how the particular move or technique can be applied to a range of cases. The hardest move is the move from a textbook example to the one you encounter in life.

As I emphasise throughout the book, clear thought requires sensitivity to the particular case and the context in which it is encountered.

How to use this book

If you passively absorb the contents of this book you probably won't dramatically improve your ability to think clearly; the whole point is to apply the ideas to new cases. The book can be read from cover to cover, dipped into and mulled over or else kept on a shelf for reference. Probably the best way to use it is to find an entry that interests you, then follow through the cross-references; this will give you a sense of the interrelation of the topics.

One of the most important steps towards becoming a better thinker is being able to identify the various moves in argument and this is made much easier when you have names to attach to them. I have tried to pick on the most memorable names for each of the topics discussed, avoiding Latin wherever possible (traditional Latin terms are cross-referenced to their nearest English equivalents). Any word in bold type signals that there is an entry on this topic, located alphabetically.

A note on the second edition

For the second edition I have added the following new entries: **Catch-22**, **circular definition**, **conditional statements**, **contraries**, **counter-example**, **domino effect**, **disanalogy**, **exception that proves the rule**, **family resemblance term**, **hypothesis**, **imply/infer**, **Ockham's razor**, **paradox**, **Socratic fallacy**, **'that's a value judgement'** and **truth by adage**. I have also added new cross-references, revised and expanded some existing entries and updated the further reading.

A note on the third edition

For the third edition I have added the following new entries: **principle of charity, lawyer's answer, least worst option, poisoning the well,**

sentimentality, sunk cost fallacy, weasel words and **'you would say that wouldn't you'**. Since the publication of the second edition, numerous books on various aspects of critical thinking have been published. Some of them are very good. I've updated the further reading by including several of these. I have also listed a number of useful web resources, though these are liable to change.

Further reading

There are a number of books which purport to give a thorough grounding in critical thinking. Unfortunately many of them demonstrate their authors' limited ability to think critically. There are, however, some notable exceptions: I recommend the following, all of which I have found useful in writing this book.

Irving M. Copi and Carl Cohen, *Introduction to Logic* (10th edition, New Jersey: Prentice Hall, 1998). An outstanding logic textbook which comes with a CD-Rom. It manages to be clear, interesting and thorough, drawing on a very wide range of examples. Although principally an introduction to formal logic it also includes substantial sections on critical thinking of the kind the present book explores.

Alec Fisher, *The Logic of Real Arguments* (Cambridge: Cambridge University Press, 1988)

Anthony Flew, *Thinking about Thinking* (London: Fontana, 1975)

Oswald Hanfling, *Uses and Abuses of Argument* (Milton Keynes: Open University Press, 1978). This was part of the Open University Arts Foundation Course, A101. It may be available from libraries.

J. L. Mackie, 'Fallacies' entry in Paul Edwards (ed.), The *Encyclopedia of Philosophy* (London: Macmillan, 1967)

Anne Thomson, *Critical Reasoning* (London: Routledge, 1996). The exercises in this book are particularly useful for developing thinking skills. For the application of these skills to ethical issues, see her *Critical Reasoning in Ethics* (London: Routledge, 1999).

R. H. Thouless, *Straight and Crooked Thinking* (revised edn, London: Pan, 1974)

Douglas N. Walton, *Informal Logic* (Cambridge: Cambridge University Press, 1989)

Anthony Weston, *A Rulebook for Arguments* (second edition, Indianapolis: Hackett, 1992). This is a good brief introduction.

Jamie Whyte, *Bad Thoughts: A Guide to Clear Thinking* (London: Corvo Books, 2003). A lively, wide ranging, and very readable book.

A more advanced book, which I have also found useful, is C. L. Hamblin's *Fallacies* (London: Methuen, 1970).

There are numerous internet sites relating to critical thinking. I've listed several here, but their content may change, and they may even close down. At the time of writing, one of the most useful online directories of relevant websites is *Critical Thinking on the Web* <www.austhink.org/critical>. Other sites you may want to look at include *The Fallacy Files* <www.fallacyfiles.org> and *A Skeptic's Dictionary* <www.skepdic.com>. My own weblog, *Virtual Philosopher* <www.virtualphilosopher.org>, includes links to critical thinking websites which I will endeavour to keep updated.

There are also a number of websites that provide stimulating and vigorously argued comments on contemporary events, such as *Butterflies and Wheels* <www.butterfliesandwheels.com>, *Edge* <www.edge.org> and *Arts and Letters Daily* <www.artsandlettersdaily.com>.

If you are interested in learning about philosophy, my books *Philosophy: the Basics* (fourth edition, Abingdon: Routledge, 2004) and its companion volume *Philosophy: Basic Readings* (second edition, Abingdon: Routledge, 2004) are intended for those who have not studied the subject before, as is my *Philosophy: the Classics* (third edition, Abingdon: Routledge, 2006); they all have detailed suggestions for further reading. My book *The Basics of Essay Wrting* (Abingdon: Routledge, 2006) includes some suggestions on how to achieve clarity.

A

absurd consequences move

Proving that a position is false, or at least untenable, by showing that if true it would lead to absurd consequences. This is sometimes called a *reductio ad absurdum*. It is a common and highly effective method of refuting (see **refutation**) a position.

For example, if someone asserts (see **assertion**) that anyone who takes a mind-altering drug is a danger to society and should be locked away, then it is easy to refute them by using an absurd consequences move. Alcohol is a mind-altering drug that many of the greatest contributors to western civilisation have used on occasion. Are we then to lock away everyone who has ever used alcohol? Clearly that would be absurd. So, we can be confident that the generalisation which led to the conclusion that we should do so is untenable. It at least has to be refined so that it is clear precisely which mind-altering drugs are supposed to be covered by the term (but see *ad hoc* **clauses**).

Consider another example. A politician might argue that a good way of increasing the income to the treasury would be to investigate every taxpayer's tax returns thoroughly, thereby clamping down on tax evasion. However, in practice this would cost far more to carry out than could possibly be reclaimed and so can be seen to lead to the absurd consequence that a scheme for increasing income would end up by reducing it. This gives us good grounds for jettisoning the politician's suggestion as matters now stand (assuming, of course, that the sole reason for implementing such a policy was to increase treasury income). If a cheaper way of investigating tax returns could be developed then the politician's suggestion might not lead to absurd consequences and could be a viable policy.

One problem with using the absurd consequences move is that there is usually no touchstone for absurdity; one person's absurdity is another's common sense. Unless a view implies a **contradiction** there is no easy way of demonstrating its absurdity (see **biting the bullet**). Nevertheless, if you can see that obviously absurd consequences follow from a position, it gives you good grounds for rejecting it.

adage

See **truth by adage**.

ad hoc clauses

Clauses added to a **hypothesis** to make the hypothesis consistent with some new observation or discovered fact. If your hypothesis is threatened by some inconvenient fact which it is incapable of explaining, you have two options: you can either abandon your hypothesis and seek a new one which *is* capable of explaining this new fact; or else you can add a special clause to your general hypothesis, an *ad hoc* clause. Patching up a hypothesis is a move which can be acceptable, but often is not. This is most clearly seen by considering examples.

A politician might claim that if the rich are encouraged to grow richer then the poorest of the nation will benefit because the wealth that the rich generate will gradually trickle down to the poor. For the sake of argument, suppose (see **supposition**) that a five-year study showed that no such trickle-down effect occurred. The politician might then be expected to abandon the initial hypothesis. However, another option would be to add a special clause to the hypothesis to prevent the evidence presented by the study standing as a **refutation** of it. For instance, the new hypothesis could be, 'If the rich are encouraged to grow richer then the poorest of the nation will benefit because the wealth that the rich generate will gradually trickle down to the poor, *but the effects of this will not be visible in the first five years.*' If the country in question was just coming out of a recession, a different *ad hoc* clause could be appended: '*but the effects of encouraging the rich to become richer will be masked by the effects of a recession.*'

A biologist might begin with the hypothesis that all independent living organisms are either unicellular (consist of a single cell) or multicellular (have many cells). However, the existence of a bizarre animal, known as slime mould, confounds this hypothesis, revealing it as a **false dichotomy** since at one stage slime mould is an independent unicellular organism and at another stage of its development it combines with other unicellular slime moulds to form a multicellular organism. The existence of slime mould confounds the hypothesis. In the light of this, the biologist might modify the initial hypothesis to, 'All independent living organisms *except slime mould* are either unicellular or multicellular.' This would be an acceptable modification; however, if there were a large number of species which, like slime mould, defied the simple dichotomy in the hypothesis then adding further *ad hoc* clauses would at a certain point undermine the power of the generalisation.

There is a fine line between making a hypothesis more detailed in the light of further evidence and undermining its power as a generalisation by adding numerous exception clauses.

ad hominem move

A Latin phrase meaning 'to the person'. It is used in two main ways, which can lead to confusion (see **ambiguity**). By far the most common use is to draw attention to the devious move in debate which I discuss in the section **getting personal**, that is, shifting attention from the point in question to some non-relevant aspect of the person making it. Calling someone's statement *ad hominem* in this sense is always a reproach; it involves the claim that the aspects of the arguer's personality or behaviour which have become the focus of discussion are irrelevant to the point being discussed.

For example, someone might argue that we shouldn't take seriously the findings of a medical scientist who had researched the beneficial effects of jogging on the cardiovascular system on the grounds that the scientist was overweight and probably couldn't run more than a hundred yards. However, this fact is entirely irrelevant (see **irrelevance**) to the scientist's ability to assess the evidence. If the scientist had been shown to be a liar, or an incompetent researcher, then that would be relevant to our understanding of the results of the research. But to focus on the scientist's level of fitness is an example of an *ad hominem* move in the first sense. This should not be confused with the charge of **hypocrisy**, not practising what you preach. The sedentary scientist would only be a hypocrite if he or she urged others to take up jogging.

An *ad hominem* argument in the second sense is a legitimate demonstration of an opponent's **inconsistency**. This is a much rarer use of the term. An argument is *ad hominem* in this second sense if it involves turning the argument back on the opponent (sometimes known as the 'you too' or '*tu quoque*' move). For instance, if someone argues both that all killing is morally wrong and that there is nothing immoral about capital punishment, then (provided that you can demonstrate that capital punishment is a form of killing — not a difficult task), you can use an *ad hominem* argument (in the second sense) in response. It is impossible without contradicting yourself (see **contradiction**) to claim that all forms of killing are morally wrong *and* that one form of killing is not morally wrong. That is tantamount to saying both that all killing is morally wrong and that it is not true that all killing is morally wrong. In this case turning the argument back on the opponent would clearly demonstrate that his or her position was untenable.

It is important to distinguish the two senses of *ad hominem* because the first is an **informal fallacy**; the second a perfectly acceptable move in argument.

affirming the antecedent

A valid **argument** (see **validity**) with the following form:

> If p then q
> p
> Therefore q

Here p and q are used to stand for any states of affairs that you care to insert: the antecedent is p and the consequent q. This form of argument is often known by its Latin name, *modus ponens*, which means 'the mood that affirms'. An example of affirming the antecedent is

> If you have bought this book I will receive a royalty.
> You have bought this book.
> Therefore I will receive a royalty.

Another example of affirming the antecedent is

> If you are a goldfish then you can ride a bicycle
> You are a goldfish
> Therefore you can ride a bicycle

Note that in this second example the obvious absurdity of the first **premise** doesn't affect the validity of the argument: both arguments have the same logical form.

Affirming the antecedent should be clearly distinguished from the **formal fallacy** known as **affirming the consequent**.

affirming the consequent

A **formal fallacy** which may have the superficial appearance of a valid argument (see **validity**). It has the following underlying form:

> If p then q
> q
> therefore p

For instance, both of the following have the same underlying structure as I have given in terms of p and q above:

> If you possess a Green Card you can work legally in the United States.
> You can work legally in the United States.
> So you've got a Green Card.

and

> If a car runs out of fuel it stops.
> Your car has stopped.
> So your car has run out of fuel.

It is probably easier to see what is wrong with this form of argument by considering some more examples of the same form:

> If she secretly loved me and didn't want her boyfriend to find out then she wouldn't reply to my letters.
> She hasn't replied to my letters.
> So she secretly loves me and doesn't want her boyfriend to find out.

What is wrong with this argument is that even if the two **premises** are true, then the conclusion isn't necessarily true: it might be true and it might not. So it's not a reliable **deduction**. Its conclusion is a ***non sequitur***: it doesn't *necessarily* follow. It treats the fact of her not replying to my letters as a sufficient condition (see **necessary and sufficient conditions**) of her secretly loving me and not wanting her boyfriend to find out. But it is obvious that the first premise does not maintain that the only possible reason for her lack of response is that she secretly loves me; for the argument to be valid we would have to read 'if' as meaning 'if *and only if* (sometimes written by logicians as 'iff'), and in most contexts it would be a sign of delusion or at least

wishful thinking to believe that the first premise offers the only possible explanation of her lack of response. There are numerous **alternative explanations** for her silence: she might be irritated by my letters, she might not want to encourage me, she might never have opened them. There is nothing inconsistent (see **consistency**) about believing both that if she secretly loves me and doesn't want her boyfriend to find out then she won't reply to my letters *and* that the fact that she hasn't replied to my letters is not necessarily an indication that she secretly loves me.

Another example. People who have AIDS are prone to colds and often suffer from night sweats. But it would be a mistake to think that just because you are prone to colds and suffer from night sweats that you must have AIDS. That is only one possible explanation; it in no way follows logically from the premise 'If you have AIDS then you will be prone to colds and may suffer from night sweats' that anyone who has these symptoms *must* have AIDS. To arrive at that conclusion you would need to believe that *only* people who have AIDS are prone to colds and nights sweats; and that is obviously untrue.

A more exaggerated example makes it clear that this form of argument is not a reliable one. It is undoubtedly true that if I had bought a new car then I would be massively overdrawn at the bank. As it happens, I *am* massively overdrawn; but there are numerous alternative explanations for this phenomenon, such as that my publisher isn't paying me high enough royalties to support my extravagant lifestyle. I couldn't reliably conclude from the fact that I am overdrawn that I must have bought a car. That would clearly be absurd. This technique of considering an obviously absurd argument of the same form in order to show the invalidity of a type of argument is a useful one; it helps separate the possible distraction of the particular content of an argument from the underlying structure. If the argument is an invalid one, even if it happens to yield a true conclusion, then we should not rely on it since the conclusion is not one that follows logically from the premises (see **bad reasons fallacy**).

One reason why fallacy of affirming the consequent can be tempting is that it superficially resembles a valid form of argument known as **affirming the antecedent** (*modus ponens*):

> If *p* then *q*
> *p*
> therefore *q*

An argument with this form is:

> If you burp your baby after feeding she'll sleep soundly.
> You have burped your baby after feeding.
> So she'll sleep soundly.

Here if the premises are true, the conclusion must be true. The fallacious form of this argument would be:

> If you burp your baby after feeding she'll sleep soundly.
> Your baby is sleeping soundly.
> So you must have burped her.

But, as the earlier examples demonstrated, affirming the consequent in no way guarantees a true conclusion even if the premises are true.

Even though many instances of this fallacy are simple to spot, when some of the premises are implicit rather than stated the reasoning errors can be harder to identify.

all and some

See **some/all confusion**.

alternative explanations

Ignored explanations of the phenomenon in question. In many situations it is tempting to believe that because an explanation is consistent (see **consistency**) with the known facts it must therefore be the correct explanation. This is especially tempting when the particular explanation is the one which we would most like to be true. However, this is **wishful thinking** and ignores the possibility of plausible alternative explanations of precisely the same observations.

The **formal fallacy** of **affirming the consequent** typically involves ignoring alternative explanations, as for instance in the following example:

> If you accidentally expose your film, then your photographs won't come out.
>
> Your photographs haven't come out.
>
> So you must have accidentally exposed your film.

Here the numerous alternative explanations for the photographs' not coming out have been completely ignored: you could have had faulty film, they could have been inexpertly developed, or perhaps you forgot to remove the lens cap.

When people are arguing from the existence of a correlation to a conclusion about a causal connection (see **correlation = cause confusion**) they are particularly prone to neglect the possibility of alternative explanations. For instance, a scientist attempting to show that musical ability is largely inherited might examine the musical ability of a large number of children of talented musicians and compare this with the ability of children from non-musical families. It would not be surprising in such a survey to discover a significant correlation between being a proficient musician and one or both of your parents being musical themselves. However, if the scientist were to take this as firm evidence of *inherited* musical ability this would be an unreliable conclusion to draw from this evidence alone, since children of musicians are far more likely to be taught to play a musical instrument from an early age than are other children. In other words, the scientist would be ignoring an alternative explanation of the same phenomenon. In fact, probably the most plausible explanation is that there are both hereditary and environmental factors in musical ability; this too is consistent with the observed facts in the imaginary case above.

People who believe that aliens from another galaxy regularly visit the earth, occasionally abduct people in order to perform medical experiments on them, buzz unsuspecting airline pilots and so on, usually maintain their exotic beliefs by ignoring the alternative explanations of the phenomena they take to be evidence for their beliefs. So, for instance, although it is undoubtedly true that strange patterns are sometimes found in cornfields, it doesn't follow that they *must* have been made by extraterrestrials. There is a wide range of far more plausible alternative explanations of the phenomenon, such as that they have been made by pranksters, or are the result of freak weather conditions. It is a huge and unwarranted step to move from the fact that such crop circles *could* have been caused by extraterrestials to the conclusion that they *must* have been. Before reaching that conclusion you would have to prove that visits by extraterrestials are the only possible explanation, or at least the most plausible one, for crop circles. Only when we have eliminated other possible explanations should we believe the improbable. And even then we should be aware of the power of wishful thinking.

ambiguity

An ambiguous word or phrase has two or more meanings. Ambiguity should not be confused with **vagueness**. Vagueness results from imprecision in language; ambiguity only arises when a word or phrase can be interpreted in different ways. There are three common sorts of ambiguity: *lexical*, *referential* and *syntactical*.

Lexical ambiguity occurs when a word with two or more possible meanings is used so that the phrase or sentence in which it appears can be understood in more than one way. For instance, a book called *The Myth of the Goddess* could either be about a particular myth or else be an attack on the idea that there ever was a goddess; this is because the word 'myth' has two related yet distinct meanings. Or, similarly, from the title *Discrimination* alone it would be impossible to tell whether a book was about the unfair treatment of certain groups in society, as in the phrase 'racial discrimination', or the ability to make subtle aesthetic judgements, as in 'the connoisseur exercised fine discrimination'. Of course both these book titles could be deliberate puns. Puns play on lexical ambiguities. When Dr Johnson saw two women standing on their doorsteps arguing he commented that they would never agree because they were 'arguing from different premises', a witticism playing on two possible meanings of 'premises'. Actually, however, two people arguing from different **premises** (in the sense of starting-points in arguments) *could* reach the same conclusion; but they wouldn't arrive at this conclusion by the same route.

Referential ambiguity occurs when a word is used so that it could be taken to be referring to either of two or more things. For instance, if two people in the room are called John, then just saying 'There's a phone call for John' will be decidedly unhelpful unless it's clear from the context which John you mean (you might, for example, look straight at the appropriate John as you say it). Such ambiguities of reference often occur when using pronouns such as 'it', 'her', 'him' and 'they'. 'The sultana rolled off my plate and came to rest underneath my fork, so I picked it up' doesn't make absolutely clear what it was that I picked up. Was it the sultana, the fork, or possibly, though less likely, the plate? (Although strictly speaking the word 'sultana' could mean 'female sultan', the context within the sentence rules out any *lexical ambiguity*.)

Syntactical ambiguity, sometimes called *amphiboly*, occurs when the order of words allows two or more interpretations. For instance, 'a small fish packing factory' could mean either a factory for packing small fish, or else a small factory for packing fish of an undisclosed size. Here judicious use of hyphens would remove the ambiguity; in other cases paraphrasing may be necessary. 'I heard about what you got up to at work yesterday' is ambiguous in two ways. It could either mean that I heard what you got up to when you were at work, or that I was at work when I heard what you got up to. The second way in which it is ambiguous is that the order of words leaves it unclear as to whether it was yesterday that I heard about you, or whether what I heard about you referred to something that you did yesterday.

While it is extremely difficult to eliminate all ambiguity, wherever there is a serious possibility of confusion it is worth taking the time to make your intended meaning clear (see also **equivocation**). However, it would be sheer **pedantry** to waste your life ruling out all possible but highly unlikely interpretations, unless of course you are drawing up a legal document.

amphiboly

See **ambiguity**.

analogy, arguments from

Arguments based on a comparison between two things which are alleged to be similar. Arguments from analogy rely on the principle that if two things are similar in some known respects they are likely to be similar in other respects even if these are not directly observable. This principle, which relies on **induction,** at best usually only yields *probable* conclusions; it rarely provides a conclusive proof since similarity in some respects does not always reliably indicate similarity in other respects. An exception to this is when the similarity in question is similarity of logical form, in which case, if one argument is valid (see **validity**), then any other argument of the same logical form must also be valid.

Arguing on the basis of analogy may at first glance seem an entirely reliable form of reasoning. How else could we learn from our experience if not by transferring the results of particular discoveries to similar new situations? However, arguments from analogy are only reliable if the situations being compared are *relevantly* similar, and unfortunately there is no simple test for relevant similarity.

One of the most famous uses of argument from analogy is the attempt to prove God's existence known as the Argument from Design. In its simplest form this is the argument that because there are various visible similarities between natural objects and those which have been designed by human beings — between the human eye and a camera, for instance — we can conclude that both must have been produced by a similar sort of intelligence. In other words, perceivable similarities between two sorts of thing are taken as a reliable indication that they have similar sorts of origin: in this case an intelligent designer. Because the eye is more sophisticated in 'design' than the camera, using this argument from analogy, we can conclude that the designer of the eye was correspondingly more intelligent and powerful than the designer of the camera. The conclusion of the Argument from Design is that the intelligent and powerful designer of the eye must have been God.

However, as many philosophers have pointed out, the analogy between such things as an eye and a camera is relatively weak; although there are respects in which they are quite similar (both have a lens, for instance), there are also numerous respects in which they differ (the eye, for instance, is part of a living organism; the camera is a machine). If the Argument from Design rests on a relatively weak analogy (see **disanology**), then its conclusions about the causes of the apparent design of natural objects must be correspondingly weak. Besides, in this case there is also a highly plausible **alternative explanation** of precisely the same observations, namely Charles Darwin's theory of evolution by natural selection. The Argument from Design does not on its own provide anything like a proof of God's existence both because the analogy on which it rests is relatively weak and because there is a competing theory which explains the apparent design of living organisms as arising from the impersonal workings of heredity and environment.

The philosopher Judith Jarvis Thomson, writing on the morality of abortion, used an analogy to defend her view that even if a foetus has rights, these do not necessarily override a woman's right to determine what happens in and to her body (see also **thought experiment**). She compared some kinds of pregnancy with the imagined situation of waking up to find that you have had a famous violinist plugged into your vital organs and being told that unless you leave him plugged in for nine months, thereby causing you considerable discomfort, he will die. The point of this far-fetched analogy was to bring out in a clear way some of what is at stake in debates about a foetus's right not to be aborted. Whilst we would admire someone who chose to keep the violinist plugged in, it does not seem accurate to say that any right he has to life overrides your right to determine what happens to your body. Obviously this is a controversial analogy which is only relevantly similar to *some* forms of pregnancy (and for most of us, the power of the thought experiment depends on knowing *which* famous violinist is to be plugged into us). However, Thomson's use of this analogy was very important in bringing out what was implicit in the pro- and anti-abortion arguments and has been the starting-point for most discussion of the topic since she published it in an article in 1971.

When animal rights activists argue that we should be more concerned about animal welfare their arguments usually rely on an implicit analogy between human and animal abilities to feel pain. We know that humans feel pain and that, in its extreme forms, it is a terrible thing which we would do almost anything to avoid: that's why torture can be so effective. Mammals are very like human beings in many ways. They are genetically quite closely related to us and have similar physiological responses to physical damage; like us they try to avoid damage to themselves, and in certain circumstances make noises which we think we can recognise as indicating that they are in pain because they are similar to noises we make when in pain. So it seems reasonable to conclude on the basis of the analogy between human beings and mammals that mammals are capable of feeling certain sorts of pain. True, there are some differences between humans and other mammals. Apart from a few exceptional chimpanzees, other mammals don't have language, for instance. But these are not usually considered relevant differences. Insects, however, are far less like most human beings than are mammals; so any conclusion about insect pain based on an analogy with human pain would be correspondingly weaker than one about mammal pain.

Consider one more example. Some pundits have argued that outlawing possession of guns in the United States would, far from reducing violent crime, actually increase the number of shootings that would occur. Their reasoning is based on the fact that outlawing alcohol during the Prohibition was correlated with a huge increase in illegal alcohol-related crime (but see **correlation = cause confusion**). Similarly, they say, outlawing gun ownership will lead to an increase in gun-trafficking, giving criminals even greater access to firearms than they now have. And the more access criminals have to firearms, the more likely they are to use them. This argument relies on there being relevant similarities between the outlawing of alcohol during Prohibition and the outlawing of guns today. It involves other **assumptions** too, such as that if criminals possess firearms they are likely to use them, and that widespread possession of firearms doesn't itself act as a deterrent to their use because of the risk of getting shot yourself if you open fire (i.e. your opponent is more likely to be armed). But the main argument rests on an analogy. However, it is fairly easy to see that this is a very weak analogy since the situations differ in so many important respects: the fact that guns don't get consumed when you use them, whereas alcohol does, for instance. If the two situations can be shown to be significantly dissimilar then any conclusions drawn on the basis of such an analogy will require independent support. The conclusion of the argument could turn out to be true (see **bad reasons fallacy**), but this argument from analogy alone does not provide conclusive support for the conclusion.

Analogies are often used as a form of **rhetoric**. When, for example, Hitler claimed that he was going to wring Britain's neck like a chicken, this was meant to show the power of Nazi Germany, and the vulnerability of Britain: Germany's relation to Britain was supposed to be like that of a farmer to a chicken about to be slaughtered. Churchill famously retorted, 'Some chicken, some neck', suggesting that the analogy was weaker in certain relevant respects than Hitler believed, and that Hitler's conclusion about the ease with which he would defeat the British and their Allies was unwarranted. Neither Hitler nor Churchill produced an argument for their conclusions.

With strong analogies, the arguer may be on safe ground. However, even where an analogy appears to be very strong, there is still a possibility of being misled. Mushrooms and toadstools can look very similar and are closely related, yet the former are edible and the latter poisonous. So even where there seem to be excellent grounds for drawing conclusions on the basis of two things being very similar in some respect, it may prove unwise to treat these conclusions as firmly established. This is not to say that arguing on the basis of an analogy should be avoided, only that it should be treated with caution and that, wherever possible, independent support for the conclusion should be sought. It would be unreasonable to expect an analogy to hold in *every* respect, or even in *most* respects; however, for the argument to have any force, the analogy must hold in *relevant* respects. What counts as a relevant respect is determined largely by context. As with most applications of critical thinking it is important to be sensitive to the particular case, a fact rarely acknowledged in textbooks on the subject.

anecdotal evidence

Evidence which comes from selected stories either of what has happened to you or to someone you know. In many cases this is very weak evidence and typically involves generalising from a particular case (see **rash generalisation**).

For instance, if you are debating whether or not acupuncture is an adequate alternative to conventional medicine, someone might tell you that their friend tried acupuncture and that it seemed to work wonders. On its own this is merely anecdotal evidence. First, there is a risk that details of the story may get changed in the retelling. More importantly, to argue from this single case that acupuncture is an adequate alternative to conventional medicine would be irresponsible: anecdotal evidence is different from a controlled scientific investigation into the effectiveness of acupuncture. For instance, a scientist investigating this question would want to have a control group to see if people spontaneously recover from ailments without having any treatment at all. A scientist would also consider more than a single case, and follow up the history of individual cases to see if any improvements in health were short-term. And, of course, comparisons would have to be made between the effects of acupuncture and more conventional medical techniques, taking into account placebo effects and the possibility of spontaneous recovery. Anecdotal evidence cannot usually provide this sort of information in a reliable form and may be clouded by **wishful thinking**.

The term 'anecdotal evidence' is often used to suggest that the evidence is *merely* anecdotal, that is, in a pejorative way. However, not all anecdotal evidence is unreliable: if you have reason to be confident in the source of the evidence, then anecdotal evidence can help to support or undermine a conclusion. Indeed, many sorts of scientific enquiry begin by examining anecdotal evidence about the phenomenon to be examined, and on the basis of this develop a way of testing in a controlled way whether or not this evidence points to the truth of the matter. For instance, an investigation into possible cures for night cramps in elderly patients might begin by looking at the anecdotal evidence that quinine in tonic water reduces their occurrence. Detailed examination of patients under controlled conditions might then reveal that the anecdotal evidence had been unreliable, and that the quinine had only a minimal effect on the incidence of cramps.

The appropriateness of using anecdotal evidence depends entirely on the context and on the type of anecdotal evidence available.

antecedent

The first part of an 'if . . . then' statement (see **conditional statement**). For example, in 'If you spend too long at the computer screen then you'll get eye strain', the antecedent is 'you spend too long at the computer screen'.

See **affirming the antecedent**, **affirming the consequent**, **consequent**, **denying the antecedent**, **denying the consequent**.

appeals to authority

See **truth by authority**.

arbitrary redefinition

See **humptydumptying** and **stipulative definition**.

argument

Reasons supporting a **conclusion**. This should not be confused with the use of 'argument', meaning a quarrel, in which **assertion** and counter-assertion are far more common than reasoning. In the sense in which 'argument' is used in this book, an argument provides reasons for believing a conclusion. In contrast, an assertion merely presents a conclusion and we have no particular grounds for believing that conclusion, unless of course we know its source to be a reliable authority on the subject of the conclusion (see **truth by authority**). Reliable authorities are usually capable of giving arguments which support their conclusions.

In logic textbooks, arguments, especially deductive ones (see **deduction**), are very neat, with the premises clearly distinguished from the conclusion and the conclusion indicated by the word 'therefore'. In real life the structure of arguments is unlikely to be so easy to identify. Usually at least one of the premises is assumed rather than stated explicitly (see **assumptions** and **enthymeme**); conclusions do not always come after the premises, they often come before, and are rarely signposted by words such as 'therefore' and 'so'. Consequently it is often necessary to clarify the precise relation between premises and conclusion before attempting to evaluate any argument.

For instance, you might come across the following:

You shouldn't let your child watch that film *A Clockwork Orange*. It's so violent.

On further questioning it might emerge that the implied argument was:

Watching violent films causes children to be violent.
You should prevent children from doing anything that makes them violent.
You can prevent your child watching a film.
A Clockwork Orange is a violent film.
Therefore you should prevent your child watching the film *A Clockwork Orange*.

This is a valid argument (see **validity**). Obviously it would in most contexts be extremely tedious to spell out every condensed argument in this fashion. However, often it is unclear precisely how the premises are supposed to be supporting the conclusion; in such cases it may be worth making the underlying argument explicit.

Notice that in the above argument, if the premises are true, then the conclusion must be true: there is no possible situation in which all the premises are true and yet the conclusion false. This is because the structure of the argument is a valid one (see **validity**). Another way of putting this is that the form of a valid argument is truth-preserving: if you put true premises into this sort of structure, then you are guaranteed to get a true conclusion from it. What's more, if you know the argument to be valid then you must either accept the conclusion as true, or else deny the truth of at least one of the premises. A valid argument with true premises is known as a **sound argument**.

Some arguments are inductive (see **induction**). For instance, consider the following:

> Picture restoration has often damaged important paintings; the world's national galleries all contain examples of damaging restoration. So you should only embark upon a policy of picture restoration with extreme caution since there is a serious risk that otherwise you will cause more damage than you prevent.

This is an argument, but it is not deductive: it is not truth-preserving. Its conclusion, that you should only embark upon a policy of picture restoration with extreme caution, is based on the evidence that some picture restorers in the past have caused serious damage to paintings. The reasons given for believing the conclusion are based on observation and on the assumption that the future will be like the past in certain relevant respects. Inductive arguments never prove anything conclusively; however they do point to what is probably or almost certainly true. They can provide very strong support for conclusions even though this always stops short of the truth-preserving nature of deductive arguments.

Arguments are of greater value than unsupported **assertion** since they provide reasoning which other people can assess for themselves to see whether or not it supports the given conclusion. Assessing the arguments on either side is one of the best methods we have for deciding between competing views on any issue. If someone presents an argument we can judge whether or not their conclusion is supported by the reasons given; if they resort to **prejudice**, **rhetoric**, and unsupported assertion, even though the conclusions may turn out to be true, we aren't in a position to see why they are true or how they have been reached.

assertion

An unsupported statement of belief. Whenever you simply say that something is the case you make an assertion.

For instance, I might say, 'Reading this book will improve your critical thinking.' This is an assertion because I have not given any reasons or evidence to support this statement. Or, I might assert 'God does not exist'; but until I offer some kind of argument or evidence, you would have no reason to believe me unless I had somehow established myself as an authority on the subject (and even then you might want to seek some kind of explanation of how I had come to this view; see **truth by authority**).

Merely asserting something, no matter how loudly, doesn't make it true. Confident assertion is no substitute for **argument**, even though most of us, in our uncritical moments, can be persuaded by people who seem to know what they're talking about, whether or not they really do. The only way other people can assess the truth of an assertion is to examine reasons and evidence that might be given in support of it, or else to seek out evidence or reasons not to believe it. Nevertheless, bald assertions of belief are common; this is in part because it would be tedious to spell out every implicit reason for holding a belief, particularly when communicating with someone who shares many of your **assumptions**.

assumption

An unstated **premise**, one that is taken for granted and never made explicit. Actually the word 'assumption' is ambiguous (see **ambiguity**) since it could also mean a stated premise that is the starting-point of an argument (see **supposition**, sometimes also known as a presupposition). We all make assumptions most of the time; if we didn't, any discussion would require so much stage-setting that we'd never get to the point. Because we share many assumptions it is relatively easy to communicate with one another. But when two people try to discuss an issue on which they hold very different assumptions, confusion and misunderstandings are likely to arise.

For instance, in a discussion about the status of so-called computer viruses, one eminent scientist argued that there are good reasons for considering computer viruses a form of life since, like ordinary viruses, they are capable of replicating themselves and are parasitic. Another scientist pointed out that even if we concede the point that computer viruses are very like ordinary viruses, this still doesn't prove that computer viruses should be considered living organisms since it is contentious to say that ordinary viruses are alive themselves. The first scientist was arguing on the basis of a strong analogy (see **analogy, arguments from**) between computer viruses and ordinary viruses and the second scientist was challenging the **conclusion** which could be drawn even if the analogy actually held. The second scientist's point was that the first scientist was making a large assumption about whether ordinary viruses are alive or not. Only if ordinary viruses were alive would the first scientist's conclusion be warranted. This assumption was not made explicit in the first scientist's argument: he only gave good reasons for there being a strong analogy between computer and ordinary viruses. Once the assumption has been made explicit it can be discussed and its truth or falsity ascertained (see also **enthymeme**). In this case the question of whether or not a virus is a living thing could be addressed and then, if this is established, the strength of the analogy between biological and computer viruses could be examined.

Some people joke that when you *assume* something you 'make an ass out of "u" and "me" '. This isn't just a bad pun; it is misleading. We all have to make assumptions most of the time and there is nothing intrinsically wrong with making them provided that the assumptions are actually true and we are aware of what those assumptions are. I suppose the point of the comment is that in certain situations it is very important not to make any assumptions before evidence has been gathered. This is very different from saying that *all* assumptions should be avoided, which would be an impossible goal (see also **some/all confusion**).

authority

See **kowtowing**, **truth by authority** and **universal expertise**.

B

bad company fallacy

Attacking another's position solely on the grounds that it is one that has also been held by some obviously evil or stupid person. This is an **informal fallacy**. The suggestion is that if someone obviously evil or stupid held that view you must be evil or stupid to hold it yourself. That this is an unreliable form of argument quickly becomes clear when you consider particular examples of it.

For instance, a scientist who after conducting many controlled experiments comes to the **conclusion** that a limited form of telepathy occurs should not dismiss these findings simply because many people believe in telepathy purely on the basis of **wishful thinking**. The scientist has evidence for his or her beliefs; the other people simply have their desire that such things occur. But the fact that they are bad intellectual company in no way undermines the scientist's **conclusion**.

A second example: if you were defending the legalisation of some forms of euthanasia and someone attempted to refute (see **refutation**) your argument by pointing out that Hitler was pro-euthanasia and brought in a euthanasia programme that resulted in the deaths of 70,000 hospital patients, they would be guilty of employing the bad company fallacy. They would also, incidentally, be guilty of equivocation since it is not at all clear that any of the so-called 'euthanasia' policies carried out by Hitler merited that name at all. They might also be using an implied **slippery slope argument**, hinting that if you legalise certain sorts of killing this will lead inexorably towards genocide. However, the bad company fallacy employed here suggests that because Hitler approved of something for that very reason it must be morally wrong or based on a false belief. This is not to say that there might not be independent reasons why legalising euthanasia might be a mistake, only that the fact that Hitler put into practice a policy of euthanasia is not in itself a good reason for avoiding doing likewise. What is needed is some kind of analysis of the relevant similarities between the two situations.

Usually those who employ the bad company fallacy do so as a form of **rhetoric** so as to persuade you that your position cannot be defended. It is particularly tempting to succumb to this rhetoric because evil and stupid people typically hold many false beliefs; also it can be extremely disconcerting to find yourself agreeing with people whom you thoroughly despise. However, that isn't enough to prove that because Hitler believed something it must therefore have been false: you need further reasons to support the claim that it is false. After all, Hitler believed that $2 + 3 = 5$ and that Berlin was in Germany. What this form of argument ignores is that evil and stupid people not only hold numerous false beliefs, but also many true ones (see also ***ad hominem* move** and **getting personal**).

The bad company fallacy is sometimes a form of **enthymeme**, that is, an argument which has an unstated **assumption** as an important **premise.** In this example the unstated assumption is 'Anything that Hitler endorsed must have been morally wrong simply because he endorsed it.' Even though Hitler endorsed many evil practices and was responsible for some of the worst known crimes against humanity, it does not follow that *everything* which he endorsed or believed was morally wrong or false.

The bad company fallacy can be contrasted with what could be called the good company fallacy: the fallacy of believing whatever someone of whom you approve endorses (see also **kowtowing**, **truth by authority** and **universal expertise**). In both cases evidence and argument should be examined, bearing in mind that even if the reasons given are poor reasons, their conclusions may still turn out to be true (see **bad reasons fallacy**).

bad reasons fallacy

The mistake of assuming that if the reasons given for a **conclusion** are false then the conclusion must itself be false. This is a **formal fallacy**. Just because someone's reasons for believing something are bad reasons it doesn't follow that what they believe is untrue. It is possible to derive true conclusions from false **premises**; it is also possible to derive them from true premises but using fallacious reasoning. Even so, it can be tempting to believe that bad arguments or false premises *never* yield truth. In fact they sometimes do; it is just that they don't *reliably* do so.

For instance, consider the following **argument**:

All fish lay eggs.
The duck-billed platypus is a fish.
Therefore the duck-billed platypus lays eggs.

This is a valid argument (see **validity**) with two false premises and a true conclusion. Premise one is false because some fish give birth to live young; premise two because the duck-billed platypus is certainly not a fish; the conclusion, however, is true since duck-billed platypuses *do* lay eggs. So in some cases a true conclusion can emerge despite the premises being false, and this means that you cannot prove a conclusion to be false simply by demonstrating that it has been derived from false premises. What you can do by this method is show that the person who holds a belief on the basis of false premises or of relying on an invalid form of argument hasn't adequately justified their belief. In this respect the situation is similar to one in which someone holds a true belief on the basis of merely **anecdotal evidence**, evidence which could nevertheless be corroborated by scientific investigation.

Take a further example, this time of an argument with a true conclusion derived from true premises but by fallacious reasoning:

> Some art galleries don't charge an entrance fee.
> London's National Gallery is an art gallery.
> Therefore London's National Gallery doesn't charge an entry fee.

The premises of this argument are true; and it is true that London's National Gallery doesn't charge an entry fee. Yet this conclusion does not reliably follow from the premises since they leave open the possibility that London's National Gallery might charge an entry fee. In other words the 'therefore' is an example of the **spurious 'therefore'** (see also *non sequitur*). All that the first premise tells us is that some art galleries are free; it gives no clues as to whether or not London's National Gallery falls within the class of free galleries. This is a weakness in the way the conclusion has been reached. You would be committing the bad reasons fallacy if you thought that by undermining the way the conclusion was reached you had demonstrated it to be false: true conclusions can be reached accidentally, or asserted without appropriate supporting evidence.

Two further examples. A poorly conducted piece of sociological research designed to assess the causes of criminal behaviour might, despite being based on an unrepresentative sample and inappropriate statistical tests, turn up some true conclusions. Someone who knows next to nothing about computers might correctly identify that your disk drive is faulty even though the way they arrived at this conclusion involved all kinds of reasoning errors. Poor reasoning in no way guarantees false conclusions. So, in order to refute (see **refutation**) a conclusion it is not enough simply to show that it has been reached by unreliable means; you need to provide further argument that demonstrates that it is false.

begging the question

Assuming the very point that is at issue. Sometimes this involves incorporating the **conclusion** of the **argument** into one of the **premises.** Often it involves circularity (see **circular arguments**). This is a valid form of argument (see **validity**) and not a **formal fallacy**: if the premises are true, then the conclusion must be true. However, since begging the question involves assuming the very point that is at issue it is a move which should not convince someone for whom that point is as yet undecided. It is uninformative and irritating rather than logically invalid.

For example, in a law case, if someone is being tried on an accusation of murder, and has pleaded not guilty, it would be begging the question to refer to them as 'the murderer' rather than 'the accused' until their guilt had been established. This is because the point of the law case is to establish whether or not they are guilty and to call them 'the murderer' would be to assume a position on the very point that is at issue. In a different context using the term would not beg any question.

The philosopher René Descartes has sometimes, controversially, been accused of begging the question with his famous *cogito* argument: 'I think therefore I am.' Since this is supposed to show that I exist, to say 'I think' assumes already that I exist and so assumes an answer to the very point that is at issue. All Descartes should have said, according to his critics, was 'there are thoughts now'; but if he had said that, it would have been difficult for him to conclude 'I exist' unless he assumed that all thoughts must have a thinker. However, to be fair to Descartes, he did explicitly deny that 'I exist' was intended to be the conclusion of a **deduction**. His point was that it was psychologically impossible to doubt the truth of the thought. So, perhaps the criticism that he was begging the question is levelled at a **straw man**.

Some forms of begging the question occur in the way questions are asked. **Complex questions** are often question-begging in this way. For instance, the question 'When did you start beating your husband?' might be question-begging if the fact that you did beat your husband had yet to be established. Or if a relation asks you what you intend to study at university, if it has yet to be established that you intend to go to university then it would be fairer to break the question down into its constituent parts: 'Do you intend to go to university?' and 'If so, what do you intend to study there?' Asking the complex question would otherwise be a case of begging the question.

This all makes it sound as if question-begging is relatively easy to spot; however, in many cases it is not obvious what is to be established. The first stage in such cases is to eliminate any lack of clarity about what is being discussed and to make explicit the point of the discussion. Only when this has been clarified is it possible to assess the extent to which the question has been begged.

There is a colloquial use of 'begging the question' with which this should not be confused. Some journalists use the phrase to mean something like 'invites the question . . .' as in, for instance, 'The difficulty of disposing of radioactive waste *begs the question* "Is nuclear power really as safe and economical as we've been told?" ' or 'The widespread corruption in the public services *begs the question* "Why hasn't there been an investigation of such misdemeanours before?" ' There is no need ever to use 'begs the question' in this sense as there are numerous unambiguous alternatives such as 'invites the question' or 'suggests the question'.

benefit of the doubt

See **proof by ignorance**.

bias

See **prejudice** and **vested interest**.

biting the bullet

Accepting the apparently unpalatable consequences which follow from principles which you are unwilling to jettison. This move can be very disconcerting when made in response to what you had thought was a **refutation** of an opponent's position. Typically it is unexpected and occurs when you think that you have demonstrated that a particular principle must be untenable because of the absurd or unattractive consequences which can be derived from it (see **absurd consequences move** and *reductio ad absurdum*). When someone both accepts that the proposed consequences do in fact follow, *and* is nevertheless prepared to accept those consequences it may be very difficult to carry on arguing, since at that point it becomes clear that there is very little hope of agreement in view of the fact that your fundamental **assumptions** are divided by such a gulf. The most extreme cases of biting the bullet occur when those with whom you are arguing have no qualms whatsoever about embracing contradictions. Logical arguments are unlikely to have much force with such people. Most of those who bite the bullet fall far short of embracing contradictions, however.

For instance, a strict utilitarian, that is, someone who believes that in any situation the morally right thing to do is whatever will bring about the greatest total happiness, will have to face a difficult decision on the morality of punishing innocent people. A consequence of the basic utilitarian principle is that if it could be shown that punishing an innocent person would in some circumstances bring about the most happiness of any possible action (perhaps because a majority of the public believed this person to be guilty and would get pleasure from the knowledge that he was punished), then it would be morally right in those circumstances to punish that innocent person. For most of us this would be an unpalatable consequence of the general utilitarian principle; for many people it would be sufficient to cast doubt on the truth of this simplest version of utilitarianism and might provide the impetus either to revise (see *ad hoc* **clauses**) or reject utilitarianism altogether. However, a hardline utilitarian might be prepared to bite the bullet and simply say, 'Yes, this is a consequence of my theory and I'm prepared to accept it: in some situations it may be morally right to punish an innocent person.'

Or, to take another example: someone might embrace the principle that only people who have never in their lives broken a law should be allowed to become judges. Whilst at first glance this might seem a sensible precaution to take, on reflection it becomes clear that this would in fact rule out almost all of those who are now judges, since the great majority of these will at some time have broken a speeding or parking restriction, or else have broken the law in some other minor way, though they may not have been prosecuted. A hard-liner might want to bite the bullet on this issue, nevertheless, and continue to maintain the principle, even though it would exclude almost all existing judges.

black-and-white thinking

Classifying every particular case as an example of one of two extremes when in fact there is a range of possible positions that can be occupied within the extremes. This is a variety of **false dichotomy**. Black-and-white thinking occurs when you try to make the world fit very simple preconceived categories.

For instance, to ignore the fact that there are many positions between being completely insane and being sane, treating everyone as if they must be simply one or the other would be an instance of black-and-white thinking. Someone who treated insanity as an all or nothing phenomenon would be seriously distorting the facts. There is a continuum along which all of us find ourselves (although our position on this continuum is by no means fixed for all our lives). Similarly, to say everyone is either a teetotaller or else an alcoholic would be to set up another obvious false dichotomy based on black-and-white thinking (see also **drawing a line**).

This is not to say that black-and-white thinking is always inappropriate: in some cases there really are just two positions which can be adopted. For instance, it would not be unreasonable to treat all responses given in a multiple choice mathematics test as either correct or incorrect; nor would it be inappropriate to divide runners into those who have run a mile in less than four minutes, and those who haven't. In both these examples there are not any positions which can be occupied between the two extremes. However, in cases where intermediate positions do exist, black-and-white thinking is always an oversimplification. Sometimes it is more than this: it can be used as a form of **rhetoric**, as for example in the cliché, 'If you're not for us, you must be against us', which sets up a false dichotomy of the black/white kind, ignoring the possibility of neutrality and of degrees of commitment in order to persuade the listener to take the plunge and support the cause in question.

C

caricature

See **straw man**.

Catch-22

A rule which allows you no way out, when another rule apparently does allow a way out. This gets its name from Joseph Heller's novel *Catch-22*, in which wartime pilots are desperate to be grounded so that they won't have to fly any more dangerous combat missions. There is a rule that says if someone is mad they have to be grounded. Some declare themselves mad in order to be grounded. But if someone asks to be grounded that is taken as conclusive evidence of their sanity: anyone who wants to get out of combat duty can't be mad. On the other hand, anyone who flies is surely crazy. This is Catch-22. It means that no one can actually get grounded. As Heller puts it in the novel: 'There was only one catch, and that was Catch-22 . . . If he flew them [more missions] he was crazy and didn't have to; but if he didn't want to he was sane and had to.'

Some people now use the term 'Catch-22' in a looser sense than this. They, for instance, use it to describe any tricky situation. However, it is best reserved for situations close to the one Heller describes.

The following is an example which might reasonably be described as a Catch-22 situation. Imagine that in order to get any job in publishing you have to be able to demonstrate your suitability by having relevant work experience with a publishing firm. Unless you have that kind of experience you won't be interviewed for the job. However, since the only way to get that experience is to get through a selection process which requires that you already have worked in publishing, you are faced with a Catch-22 situation. It seems that you might be able to get a job in publishing if only you could get the relevant work experience, but getting the work experience is a prerequisite which you need to work in publishing at all. So you can't get started in publishing at all.

cause and effect

See **correlation = cause confusion** and *post hoc ergo propter hoc*.

charity, principle of

Interpreting arguments or positions adopted by others in the best possible light. Rather than setting an opponent's pronouncements up as an easy target, those who adopt the principle of charity look for the best case that this person could consistently be making rather than the worst. Adopting the principle of charity is the opposite of setting up a **straw man**. Rather than caricaturing an opponent's position, charitable thinkers give everything about it the benefit of the doubt. The appropriateness of this depends entirely on the context.

Most everyday discussions are incomplete in many ways. Speakers omit key moves, or don't make their underlying **assumptions** clear, for example. Consequently, many contributions to a discussion are open to interpretation. Those who adopt the principle of charity interpret, or at times reconstruct, another's comments or ideas. There can be value in thinking about others' challenges and arguments in their most plausible form. The process can be intellectually stimulating because it typically requires an act of creative imagination to recreate a strong argument from a series of **assertions.**

For example, in a debate about animal welfare, a speaker might state that all animals should be given equal rights. One response to this would be that that would be absurd, because it would be nonsensical, for example, to give giraffes the right to vote and own property since they would not understand either concept. A more plausible interpretation might be to take 'All animals should be given equal rights' as a shorthand for 'All animals should have equal rights of protection from harm' and then to address that. Someone who adopted the principle of charity here would be forced to think through the strongest form of this argument rather than be satisfied with an easily refuted (see **refutation**) straw man. The process may result in a more stimulating discussion than if the speaker had simply refuted his or her opponent with a **knock-down argument**.

One problem with this approach, however is that it might simply be an intellectual exercise. There is no guarantee that your opponent would really want to defend the reconstructed argument, so the charitably interpreted argument may be the wrong argument to consider altogether if you are trying to engage with another person's actual thought rather than an idealised version of it. And even when put in their strongest form, arguments may still be open to counter-argument, or refutation.

There is no obligation to adopt a principle of charity, and in many cases it would be entirely inappropriate, labour-intensive, and unrewarding. But it can provide an occasional antidote to knocking down straw men, and to the kind of relentless negativity that clear thinkers are sometimes accused of.

circular arguments

A circular argument takes the form:

> *A* because of *B*
> *B* because of *A*

When there is no independent reason for believing *A* or *B*, then this is described as *viciously circular* and should be rejected as a particularly unenlightening form of **begging the question**. If there is no further support for *A* or *B* then it is equivalent to the impossible pastime of lifting yourself off the ground by pulling on both your shoelaces.

For instance, if someone tells you that there must be a God because the Bible or some other holy book says that God exists, and then, when asked how we know that what is written in the holy book is true replies that it must be true because it is the word of God, then this would be a viciously circular way of arguing. If there is independent proof that whatever is written in the holy book is true, or perhaps some other independent proof of God's existence, then we would have reasons which support the conclusion but which are not obviously presupposed in the conclusion. As the argument stands, however, it would be totally unconvincing to an agnostic or atheist since it assumes that God exists, or that what is written in the holy book is true, both of which are major points at issue in such a discussion.

A more complex and controversial philosophical example occurs in some attempts to justify **induction**. Induction is the method of reasoning which moves from a number of particular **empirical** observations to a general conclusion. For example, when, on the basis of biting into a large number of lemons, I conclude that all lemons are bitter, I reason inductively. However, this form of reasoning is hard to justify since however many lemons I bite into (short of managing to bite every lemon that exists or will ever exist) it is still possible that not all lemons are bitter: how can I be so sure that the next lemon I bite into won't be sweet? One attempt to justify induction is to suggest that we know it is a reliable way of arguing because it has worked well for us in the past: we have all made a large number of successful inductive generalisations before now, so we can conclude that it is a reliable way of reasoning. However, on closer inspection this turns out to be a circular argument. To appeal to past observations of induction working is to rely on induction about the past success of induction; we could only do this if we knew that induction was a reliable method of reasoning.

Circular arguments are not invalid; in other words, from a logical point of view there is nothing intrinsically wrong with them. However, they are, when viciously circular, spectacularly uninformative.

circular definition

This occurs when whatever is to be defined (the *definiendum*) itself crops up in the definition (the *definiens*). The point of defining a term is to explain its meaning; this obviously cannot be achieved if you need already to understand the meaning of the term in order to understand the definition. Circular definitions, then, miss the point of definition.

For example, to define 'philosophy' as 'the activity carried out by philosophers' would be to give a circular definition if there were no obvious independent way of working out what makes a philosopher a philosopher apart from the fact that he or she engages in philosophical activity. To define 'stress' as 'the physiological and psychological responses to stressful situations', would, similarly, be to give a circular definition. This is because stressful situations are presumably only recognisable from the fact that they tend to produce stress: but the meaning of 'stress' is the very thing which someone requesting the definition is seeking to understand, and so should not be presupposed in the definition.

coincidence

See **correlation = cause confusion**.

companions in guilt move

Demonstrating that the case in question is not unique. This is usually intended to dilute the force of an argument by showing that demands of **consistency** should lead the arguer to apply the same principles in further cases, something that he or she may not want to do. The companions in guilt move amounts to pointing out that if the arguer really wants to defend the conclusion given then he or she will have to **bite the bullet** and accept that further cases will have to be treated in the same way, or else explain what it is about the present case that makes it different from other cases which appear to share the relevant features.

For instance, if you believe that professional boxing should be banned because it sometimes results in horrific injuries and even death, then a defender of the sport might point out that boxing is not a special case in this respect. Motor racing, cricket, rugby, karate and powerboat racing also sometimes result in horrific injuries, and are thus, in this respect, companions in guilt with boxing. To be consistent the opponent of boxing would need to adopt the same stance towards all these other sports, or else show how they are relevantly different from boxing. Of course, there might be such reasons: one reason often given for singling out boxing is that it is one of very few sports in which actual physical damage to your opponent is one of the principal aims. Using the companions in guilt move may force your opponent to be explicit about what he or she takes to be unique to the topic in question.

Consider another example, a more literal example of companions in guilt. When Jesus prevented a mob from stoning a woman caught in adultery he used the ploy of suggesting that whoever among them was without sin should cast the first stone. The idea was that if the woman was guilty of sin, then so too was everyone in the crowd. But it is possible that the sins that some of the people about to stone the woman were of a sufficiently different kind (sins of thought, perhaps, rather than of action) to set them apart from the woman, and that they could have made a case for the woman's sins being of a more serious nature than their own (though not, presumably, so serious as to justify the cruel practice of stoning).

Some uses of the companions in guilt move are dubious. For instance, some people use it to excuse bad behaviour on the grounds that other people also behave badly (see **'everyone does it'**).

comparing like with like

See **analogy, arguments from** and **disanalogy**.

complex questions

Questions with several parts but which have the appearance of simple questions. The use of complex questions is sometimes known as the fallacy of many questions (an **informal fallacy**). Complex questions usually involve **begging the question** since they typically assume a position on the very point that is at issue. It is extremely difficult to answer them in a straightforward way without seeming to accept the questioner's **assumptions**. Such questions are often used deliberately to trick the unwary into some kind of confession or apparent confession.

For instance, if someone asks you, 'When did you stop taking drugs?' this may be a deliberate ploy to get you to admit by implication that you used to take drugs. If it has yet to be established that you have ever taken drugs, then it would be fairer to ask you three simpler questions which are implicitly contained in this complex question:

1. Have you ever taken drugs?
2. If so, have you stopped taking them?
3. If so, when did you stop taking them?

Until the answers to the first and second questions have been established, it would in most contexts be question-begging to ask, 'When did you stop taking drugs?'

The journalist who asks a famous author, 'When did you decide you wanted to be a novelist?' may be asking a complex question to save time. But this is clearly question-begging in that it assumes that the author actually did decide at some time to become a novelist, which needn't have been the case at all; the author might never have decided to become a novelist. The journalist's question could be broken down into simpler questions:

1. Did you make a decision to become a novelist?
2. If so, when?

In the two examples given above there is a simple way out for the person being questioned: to answer: 'I have never taken drugs' or 'I never made a conscious decision to become a novelist'. But some other forms of complex question can be much harder to answer. For instance, if someone asks, 'Are you going to carry on behaving like a spoilt brat or will you concede that you ought to spend at least half an hour a day doing the housework?' then it is almost impossible to give a brief answer without suggesting either that you have been behaving like a spoilt brat and that you will carry on doing so, or that you are prepared to concede that you ought to spend at least half an hour a day doing the housework. But the questioner may have set up a **false dichotomy**: there may be further options not given in this complex question. Saying 'I have not behaved and therefore cannot continue to behave like a spoilt brat, nor will I concede that I ought to spend at least half an hour a day doing the housework' seems a very long-winded way of answering such a question, but unless you answer the constituent parts individually, you are likely to find that you have been tricked into an implicit agreement with the questioner's **assumptions**.

Complex questions should not be confused with leading questions, although some leading questions are complex questions. Leading questions are questions which suggest the answer which the person being questioned should make. In ordinary conversation there is nothing wrong with such questions; however, they are not always permitted in a court of law.

compound questions

Another name for **complex questions**.

conclusion

The main judgement arrived at in an **argument**. Despite the name, conclusions don't necessarily conclude an argument in the sense of coming at the end; often conclusions are stated first and then reasons given in support of them.

For instance, in the following argument the conclusion is the first statement:

> The British royal family should be abolished.
> It is a symbol of inequality.
> And their marital problems set a bad example for the rest of the population.

The conclusion only follows logically if certain **assumptions** about the conditions for abolishing the monarchy are made, such as that you should abolish anything that is a symbol of inequality, or anything that sets a bad example for the rest of the population.

One of the main aims of critical thinking is to arrive at true conclusions on the basis of good reasoning from true premises (see also **sound arguments**).

conditional statements

Statements of the form 'if p then q'.

For example, the following are conditional statements:

> If the alarm is sounding someone has tried to break into your car
> If you dig the soil well then its fertility will be increased.
> If Darwin's theory of evolution is true, then we are directly descended from apes.

When a conditional statement is true, this is not because its **antecedent** is true, but rather because of the relation between the antecedent and the **consequent**. So, for example, the following is a true conditional statement, despite the fact that the antecedent is false:

> If René Descartes is still alive now then he is over four hundred years old.

A true conditional statement is one which guarantees that provided that the antecedent is true, the consequent must be true. (See also **no hypotheticals move**.)

consensus

See **democratic fallacy** and **truth by consensus**.

consequent

The second part of an 'if . . . then' statement (see **conditional statement**). For example, in 'If you spend too long in front of the computer screen then you'll get eye strain', the consequent is 'you'll get eye strain'.

See **antecedent**, **affirming the antecedent**, **affirming the consequent**, **denying the antecedent**, **denying the consequent**.

consistency

Two beliefs are consistent if they can both be true, inconsistent if only one of them can be. For instance, my belief that people who are caught drinking and driving should be severely punished and my belief that drinking alcohol tends to make people overconfident about their competence at driving are consistent since I can believe both without suggesting any **contradiction**. My beliefs that bullfighting is a cruel sport and that London is in England are also consistent, despite being completely unrelated. However, were I to believe that all destruction of fertilised human eggs is morally wrong and that the use of the intra-uterine device (the coil) is morally acceptable I would, probably unwittingly, have inconsistent beliefs. This is because the intra-uterine device frequently works by destroying fertilised eggs, rather than simply preventing eggs from being fertilised. So I would believe both that all destruction of fertilised eggs was morally wrong, and that use of a device which sometimes brought about the destruction of fertilised eggs was morally acceptable. Or to put the implicit contradiction in even starker form, I would believe that all destruction of fertilised human eggs was both always morally wrong and not always morally wrong.

Consistent application of principles means not making special exceptions without good reasons (see **companions in guilt move** and ***ad hoc* clauses**). If, for example, one country intervenes in a civil war in another one, allegedly on humanitarian grounds, consistency seem to demand that similar action be taken in any relevantly similar case. Lack of consistency might suggest that the first country had a **vested interest** in a particular outcome in the civil war in question and that the given principle was not the real reason for becoming involved, but rather a **rationalisation**.

continuum

See **black-and-white thinking**, **drawing a line** and **slippery slope arguments**.

contradiction

Two statements which cannot both be true because one denies the other. For example, I contradict myself if I say both that I have and have not been to New York. I both affirm and deny that I've been there. Any statement can be contradicted by prefixing it with the words 'It is not the case that'. (See also **consistency** and ***reductio ad absurdum*.*) It is a basic principle of logic, sometimes known as the principle of non-contradiction, that a statement cannot be both true and false at the same time.

contraries

Two statements which cannot both be true, though they can both be false. Not to be confused with a **contradiction** in which one statement is the negation of the other so that both cannot be false; nor can they both be true.

For example the statements 'rowing is the best sport for all round fitness' and 'swimming is the best sport for all round fitness' are contraries. They can't both be true, since there can only be one best sport for all round fitness. If either statement *is* true, then the other must be false. But they can also *both* be false, if, for instance, boxing turns out to be the best sport for all round fitness. The two statements above don't contradict each other. 'Rowing is the best sport for all round fitness' and 'rowing is not the best sport for all round fitness' is an example of a direct contradiction. If, however, someone accurately declares that 'swimming is the best sport for all round fitness', then this implies that rowing is not the best sport for all round fitness. Then the implied statement does contradict the statement 'rowing is the best sport for all round fitness'.

correlation = cause confusion

The mistake of treating a correlation as conclusive evidence of a direct causal connection. Two sorts of event may be correlated (that is, whenever one is found, the other is usually found) without there being a direct causal connection between them. Just because two things tend to be found together, it doesn't follow that one of them causes the other. Nevertheless many people act as if any correlation provides proof of a direct causal link. But such correlation may result from a common cause of the two events, from mere coincidence, or it may provide just as much evidence for an alternative hypothesis as it does for the one which is alleged to follow from it (see **alternative explanations**). This isn't to say that correlations are irrelevant to answering questions about causes: far from it, they are the basis of most judgements about causes. However, it is important to recognise the common errors which people make when reasoning about causes.

It is easy to find examples of correlations which are far more systematic than could occur by chance and yet which it would be absurd to treat as evidence of a direct causal link. For instance, there is a high degree of correlation between shoe size and vocabulary size: people with larger shoe sizes tend to have much larger vocabularies than people with smaller shoe sizes. But having larger feet does not *cause* anyone to gain a larger vocabulary; nor does having a large vocabulary *cause* your feet to grow. The obvious explanation of the correlation is that children tend to have much smaller feet than adults, and, because children acquire their vocabularies gradually as they grow older, it is hardly surprising that, on average, people with smaller feet have smaller vocabularies. In other words, foot size and vocabulary size can be explained in terms of features of the process of human development from infancy to adulthood: a cause which both observed phenomena have in common.

Correlations may stem from coincidence rather than causal links; this is particularly likely when there have been relatively few examples of the correlation on which to base the conclusion. For instance, a superstitious sports fan might notice that every time she wore her lucky ring, her favourite team won; when she forgot to put it on her team lost. Being superstitious, she concluded that somehow wearing the ring *caused* her team to win, when in fact it was purely coincidental, as she would no doubt have discovered if she had observed the pattern of her team's performance in relation to her ring-wearing over, say, a year. The superstitious sports fan's reasoning is an example of the reasoning error traditionally known as **post hoc ergo propter hoc** (Latin for 'because it occurs after this, therefore it occurs because of this'), a pattern of reasoning to which human beings are especially prone.

When attempting to understand the causes of various phenomena, discovering a correlation between supposed cause and effect should only be the first stage; in every case a plausible explanation of *how* the cause brings about that particular effect is needed. A healthy scepticism about causal links alleged on the basis of observed correlation is admirable, though this can be taken too far. For instance, at least one eminent scientist has attacked a very plausible hypothesis about the causal links between smoking and getting lung cancer. His grounds for this attack stem from the sort of consideration discussed above: the possibility of the two correlated phenomena having a common cause rather than one being the cause of the other. Despite the degree of correlation between being a heavy smoker and getting lung cancer in later life, and the convincing medical explanations of how this link occurs, the scientist claimed that the evidence pointed in a different direction. He maintained that people who are genetically prone to getting lung cancer are also far more likely to take up smoking.

So it isn't the smoking that causes lung cancer, but the fact that you are the type of person who is both likely to take up smoking and likely to get lung cancer that explains the observed correlation between smoking and lung cancer. It is possible that the scientist was simply playing **devil's advocate**, to get scientists to sharpen their reasoning about smoking. However, if this wasn't the case, then his alternative hypothesis should be assessed for its explanatory force and predictive ability.

counterexample

A particular case which refutes a generalisation. As generalisations can be shown to be false by means of a single exception, arguing by counterexample is a powerful tool for undermining them, and is particularly effective against **rash generalisations**.

For example, if someone made the rash generalisation 'All doctors' handwriting is illegible' then a single case of a doctor whose handwriting could be read would refute it. Such sweeping statements are an invitation to search for counterexamples. Similarly, if someone were to declare 'There have never been any great women scientists', then the mention of Marie Curie should be sufficient to refute the generalisation, without the need to list any other women scientists who could reasonably be considered great.

Assuming that the counterexample is a genuine counterexample, the only recourse of the person whose generalisation has been so conclusively refuted is either to revise or discard the generalisation. One form of revision is simply to append *ad hoc* **clauses**; this is rarely satisfactory. In many cases changing the explicit or implicit 'all' to 'some' or 'many' will make the original statement immune to the simple **knock-down arguments** provided by a single counterexample. (See also **exception that proves the rule**.)

D

deception

See **economy with the truth** and **lying**.

deduction

Valid reasoning (see **validity**) from **premises** to **conclusion**. Deductive arguments are truth-preserving, that is, if you begin with true premises the conclusion must be true. Unlike **induction**, deduction from true premises guarantees true conclusions.

For example, the following is a deductive argument:

If anyone drinks and drives they deserve to be fined.
You do drink and drive.
So you deserve to be fined.

If the premises are true, then the conclusion must be true. The conclusion brings out what is implicit in the premises. Here is another example of deduction:

> All Gods are immortal.
> Zeus is a God.
> Therefore Zeus is immortal.

Again, if the premises are true, then the conclusion must be true.

definition

See **circular definition, dictionary definition, humptydumptying, necessary and sufficient conditions, Socratic fallacy** and **stipulative definition**.

democratic fallacy

The unreliable method of reasoning which treats majority opinion as revealed by voting as a source of truth and a reliable guide for action on *every* question. This is an **informal fallacy**. Political democracy is desirable because it allows widescale political participation and can provide a valuable check on would-be tyrants. However, there are many areas of life in which taking a vote would be an extremely unreliable way of discovering the most appropriate course of action. Those who succumb to the democratic fallacy feel a need to put decisions to the vote wherever possible, naïvely assuming that this is either the best way of discovering the truth about any matter, or else the best strategy for making sensible decisions. But, obviously, if the majority of voters are largely ignorant of the matter on which they are voting, this is likely to be reflected in their voting patterns.

For instance, an airline pilot faced with the decision of whether or not to make an emergency landing because of bad weather conditions would be ill-advised to allow the passengers to vote on the issue; any majority decision would be unlikely to be based on thorough knowledge of the possible outcome and assessment of the dangers involved. It would also be an abnegation of the pilot's responsibilities to shirk the decision-making. Often those who want to put every important decision to the vote are using the democratic procedure as a way of avoiding responsibility for the decisions they make: in other words, their faith in the democratic procedure involves a kind of **wishful thinking** since it is convenient for them not to put themselves into a position of ultimate responsibility. The truth is that democracy is only of value in some contexts; in others it is completely inappropriate. What is generally needed is an *informed* majority, not simply a majority.

denying the antecedent

A **formal fallacy** with the form:

> If p then q
> not p
> therefore not q

Like the fallacy of **affirming the consequent**, it treats 'if' as if it means 'if and *only if*'. For example, the following is an example of denying the antecedent:

> If the share prices rise, then you'll get rich.
> The share prices haven't risen.
> So you won't get rich.

In this example, it is *possible* for you to get rich despite the fact that the share prices haven't risen. Rising share prices aren't the only mechanism by which people get rich.

Or consider another example:

> If you add horse manure to the soil you will increase your yield of vegetables.
> You haven't added horse manure to the soil.
> So you won't increase your yield of vegetables.

Again, adding horse manure to the soil is not the only way of increasing the yield of vegetables: you can add compost, seaweed, pig manure and all kinds of inorganic fertilisers. So the conclusion doesn't follow logically from the premises: it is a ***non sequitur***.

In some cases, the context and subject matter of the argument make it clear that 'if' is to to be understood as meaning 'if and *only if*'. These are not cases of denying the antecedent. For example, in the following, 'if' can only mean 'if and only if':

> If you have a ticket for the national lottery you'll stand a chance of winning.
> You haven't got a ticket.
> So you don't stand a chance of winning.

This is a valid argument (see **validity**) since the only way of standing a chance of winning the national lottery is by having a ticket.

denying the consequent

A valid **argument** (see **validity**) with the following form:

> If *p* then *q*
> Not *q*
> Therefore not *p*

This form of argument is often known by its Latin name, *modus tollens*. An example of denying the consequent is:

> If it rains then you'll get wet.
> You haven't got wet.
> So it's not raining.

devil's advocate

Someone who puts the strongest possible case against a position for the sake of argument rather than because of real disagreement with the position. The devil's advocate tests an opponent's argument to the limit often despite being broadly sympathetic with it. This is a useful technique for identifying loopholes and for avoiding sloppy thinking. If an argument can withstand sustained onslaught from someone scrutinising it for weaknesses then it may well be a good one; if it can't, then it should be patched up (preferably not by adding spurious *ad hoc* **clauses**), or at worst, jettisoned.

The philosopher René Descartes in his *Meditations* wanted to defend the view that there are some things which we can know for certain. However, rather than simply stating his conclusions, he began his 'First Meditation' by playing devil's advocate against his own ideas, putting forward the best case for extreme scepticism about the information we acquire through our five senses. He pointed out that everything we learn through the senses is open to doubt, not just because the senses can be unreliable, but also because we can't be certain at any particular time that we are not dreaming. He went even one step beyond this, imagining that he was being systematically deceived by a cunning and powerful evil demon (an example of a **thought experiment**), and questioned whether he could be absolutely certain that this wasn't happening to him. Only after Descartes had built up the best possible case for the idea that we can know nothing for certain did he set out his idea that the very act of doubting proves for certain that the doubter exists. Thus by first examining the best possible arguments against his own position he pre-empted many of the criticisms that sceptics would otherwise have made against his position and demonstrated the force of his anti-sceptical argument.

People who play devil's advocate are sometimes accused of **hypocrisy**, especially when they make criticisms which they do not sincerely endorse: they don't really believe in the arguments they use, or else they know the **conclusion** of the position they are attacking is true. However, this accusation of hypocrisy misses the point and perhaps in part stems from the negative associations of the word 'devil' in the title at the expense of the connotations of the word 'advocate'. Hypocrites hide their true intentions and beliefs; those who play devil's advocate openly encourage their targets to give watertight arguments for their conclusions and to take heed of the force of the strongest arguments on the other side. Often the point of using this strategy is to get someone to give good reasons in support of conclusions to which the devil's advocate is favourably disposed, thus encouraging them to investigate the justification for views which might turn out to be mere

prejudices, or perhaps true conclusions defended by weak arguments (see **bad reasons fallacy**). This, despite appearances, is not hypocrisy, but rather part of a sincere pursuit of the truth.

dictionary definitions

Accounts of how words are and have been used. Some people treat the dictionary as the ultimate judge on questions of meaning. For instance, such people will assume that the question 'What is art? can be answered by consulting the best available dictionary. But this is over-optimistic: when people ask a question such as 'What is art?' they aren't requesting information of this sort. We know roughly how people use the word 'art', but that won't solve the question of what art actually is and of whether or not certain ways of using the word can be justified. A satisfactory answer to the question will go far beyond a description of linguistic practice and, perhaps, will tell us whether we are justified in applying the word to, for example, a dead sheep suspended in a tank of formaldehyde.

A simple record of the use of particular words will be neutral on the question of whether there is an independent justification for using words in this way. What is more, dictionary definitions are usually quite short, and often somewhat vague (see **vagueness**); sometimes they merely provide synonyms or near-synonyms of the word in question. It might be tempting to begin a discussion of the nature of justice by consulting a reliable dictionary to see how the word is commonly used. But this will not answer the political philosopher's question 'What is justice?' At best it might provide a starting point for discussion. To treat the dictionary as the arbiter in debates of this kind is to give it an inappropriate authority; it involves the **assumption** that the common use of a term is the one for which there is the best justification, an assumption which is not usually warranted.

This isn't to say that the dictionary cannot be the ultimate judge on *some* questions; if you want to know how words happen to be used and how they are conventionally spelt, then this is the place to look. However, to expect a dictionary to provide answers to theoretical questions such as 'What is art?' or 'What is justice?' is a mistake. (See also **etymological fallacy**, **humptydumptying**, **Socratic fallacy** and **stipulative definition**.)

disanalogy

Way in which two things being compared in an analogy (see **analogy, arguments from**) differ. If there is a serious disanalogy then this undermines an argument from analogy.

For example, if someone attempts to persuade you that taking heroin is not significantly different from drinking an occasional glass of claret, then you can undermine their case by pointing out a number of serious disanalogies inherent in the comparison, and thereby refute their argument. First, although there are health risks attached to wine-drinking, they pale by comparison with those arising from the consumption of addictive drugs. Secondly, wine-drinking is legal, drug-taking illegal, so from a social point of view there are many far more serious consequences involved in heroin use than in alcohol consumption. These two disanalogies alone seriously weaken the analogy between heroin and claret consumption and so undermine any conclusions reached on the basis of the analogy.

The difficulty when pointing out disanalogies between two things being compared comes in deciding what is to count as a *relevant* disanalogy, since there are disanalogies to be found between any two things. Pointing out irrelevant disanalogies does not weaken an argument from analogy.

distraction

See **irrelevance, politician's answer, red herrings** and **smokescreen**.

domino effect

If one thing is allowed to happen then this will inevitably trigger a chain of subsequent undesirable events, just as if you knock over one domino then this will topple the next, which will topple the next, and so on. This metaphor is usually used rhetorically (see **rhetoric**). United States politicians famously used it during the Vietnam War to justify their country's involvement: if one state were allowed to fall to communism, then, by the domino effect, this would have an inevitable and irreversible knock-on effect with state after state falling to communism – or so it was alleged.

Clearly, though, as with the closely related **slippery slope argument**, the metaphor of the domino effect is only relevant in some cases. Any inevitability of consequence stems from the phenomenon in question and not from the label given to it. The metaphor persuades those who don't stop to think that there is an inevitable consequence of a particular action; however, in most cases where the phrase 'domino effect' is used, this is merely a technique of persuasion and no further evidence or argument is provided. Even with real dominos the domino effect doesn't always inevitably occur: a slight misalignment can lead to a break in the knock-on effect leaving some dominos standing.

As with analogies (see **analogy, argument from**), you should always be wary of implied parallels between two phenomena and investigate whether or not there are indeed relevant similarities between the two things being compared. (See also **disanalogy**.)

drawing a line

Making a distinction between two categories which only differ in degree. Where there is a continuum, such as that between rich and poor, for some purposes, such as deciding who should be eligible for tax relief, it is necessary to draw a line between what is to count as rich and what as poor. Where we draw the line might be to some extent arbitrary, but that doesn't mean that we shouldn't actually draw it. Sometimes the fact that a line could have been drawn elsewhere is taken as evidence that we should not draw a line at all, or that the line that has been drawn has no force; in most contexts this view is wrong.

Many cases of drawing the line arise in relation to the law. For example, the age of consent in Britain is fixed at 16 years, though it could have been fixed a few weeks or months earlier or later without making any significant difference. But this doesn't mean we shouldn't draw a line at all; in order to protect children from sexual exploitation it is important to fix an age beneath which sexual intercourse is prohibited by law. Similarly, in Britain the speed limit in built-up areas is 30 miles per hour; it could have been fixed at 25 miles per hour or 35 miles per hour. However, it in no way follows from this that we should ignore the speed limit once the line between speeding and driving safely has been established, nor that the arbitrariness of the precise speed at which the line was drawn means that it could just as well have been fixed at 90 miles per hour. (See also **slippery slope arguments**.)

E

economy with the truth

Selective withholding of information with intent to deceive. Some people persuade themselves that choosing not to say something incriminating is less culpable than outright **lying**. Consequently they go to great lengths to avoid saying anything that is untrue, whilst being quite content to be economical with the truth and thereby mislead other people. This is simply **wishful thinking** on their part. What is wrong with lying is not just that it typically results in people believing things which aren't true, but also that it involves deliberate deception and may have bad consequences. Yet being economical with the truth also involves deliberate deception and can have just as unpleasant consequences as lying. It is hard then to see how to justify drawing a moral distinction between the two sorts of deception. The main difference seems to be that lying is usually easier to prove than cases of being economical with the truth.

For instance, if the police were to stop your car late at night and ask you if you had been drinking that evening and you were to answer 'No, not a drop', despite the fact that you had been drinking all afternoon (but not evening), then you would be guilty of deception even though you had not lied. A man who, in answer to the question 'Have you ever been unfaithful to me?' replies to his partner 'I swear I've never had sex with another woman', and isn't lying, is being economical with the truth if he has had sex with a man, and is deliberately concealing this fact by his answer.

Being economical with the truth is very different from mere forgetfulness. The former involves a conscious attempt to mislead; the latter may reveal unconscious desires to mislead, but these desires and their expression are not of a kind for which we usually hold people responsible (see also **lawyer's answer**).

emotive language

Language which arouses emotion, usually by expressing the speaker's or writer's approval or disapproval of a person, a group of people or an activity. The typical emotions aroused by such language are hatred or strong approval, more often the former than the latter.

For instance, someone who disapproves of capital punishment might choose to describe it as 'murder'. This would be **rhetoric**, intended to persuade others of the repugnance of judicial killing, or at least to reinforce their strong feelings against it. By using the emotive word 'murder' with all its associations of brutal killing and evil, the speaker would be encouraging the audience to feel the same way about capital punishment as he or she does about unlawful killing. By arousing strong emotions, the speaker may make critical examination of the arguments for and against the practice difficult.

To call the homeless 'victims of society' expresses sympathy, and might evoke compassion in an audience; to call them 'scroungers' expresses resentment and would probably arouse or reinforce hatred towards them.

Whether you choose to call those who use violence to achieve political ends 'terrorists' or 'freedom fighters' depends entirely on whether you approve or disapprove of their aims and activities: whether you see them as allies or enemies. What is more, the label will not just express your disapproval or approval, but will also very likely arouse strong feelings in those who hear or read your words. There is no obvious neutral term for the activities of those who use violence to achieve their political goals. This isn't entirely surprising as few of us would advocate a neutral reaction to the activities of people who are prepared to maim, kill and be killed for a cause. In some cases to use non-judgmental language would be a sign of moral indifference or complacency.

However, where there is the possibility of rational discussion or negotiation between people with polarised views it is a good idea to avoid emotive language as much as possible since it often involves **begging the question** and usually only entrenches opponents in their positions. It often embodies **assumptions** which would be seen to be false if stated explicitly, but which can have persuasive force when left unstated.

Use of emotive language should not be confused with *emotivism*, which is a philosophical theory about the nature of moral judgements.

empirical

Based on experience or observation. Scientific research is empirical: it is based on evidence acquired by observation which is used to support or else to refute (see **refutation**) a hypothesis. For example, a researcher who wanted to discover whether or not a particular sleeping pill really helped insomniacs sleep would conduct an empirical test. This might involve comparing the sleep patterns of a large group of insomniacs who took the pill with a matched group of insomniacs who didn't.

(See also **anecdotal evidence**, **induction** and '**research has shown that . . .**'.)

enthymeme

An **argument** with a suppressed **premise**. In other words, it is an argument with a tacit **assumption** without which the **conclusion** would be a *non sequitur*.

For instance, consider the following:

This newspaper publishes outright lies, so it should be shut down.

The speaker of this sentence may well be putting forward an implicit argument rather than merely asserting an opinion (see **assertion**): there is an unstated premise which when added makes this a **deduction**. The structure of the argument when given in full would be:

Any newspaper which publishes outright lies should be shut down.
This newspaper publishes outright lies.
So this newspaper should be shut down.

Obviously it would have been tedious and unnecessary to trot out the whole argument and in most contexts the suppressed premise would have been fairly easily understood. However, in many cases when assumptions are not made explicit there is some scope for **ambiguity**. For instance, if someone declared:

Smoking in restaurants is unpleasant for non-smokers so it should be made illegal.

it would not be clear what the implicit premise was. It could be, 'All public activities which are found unpleasant by some people should be made illegal' (which, if taken seriously would lead to serious curtailment of individual liberty, see **companions in guilt move**); or perhaps, 'All public activities which are found unpleasant by a very large number of people should be made illegal' (this again, if applied to a range of cases, would lead to a serious curtailment of individual liberty). Perhaps here there is an implicit assumption of the known dangerous effects of passive smoking that makes outlawing smoking in restaurants a special case; or perhaps the assumed principle is that any activity, whether in private or public, which causes offence to others should be outlawed (an extreme and unworkable principle). In this sort of case it is important to clarify the concealed premise. Often speakers are somewhat unclear about what their implicit premises are; in such cases, the use of 'so' or 'therefore' may be spurious (see **spurious 'therefore' and spurious 'so'**).

equivocation

A kind of lexical **ambiguity** in which the same word or phrase is used twice or more within an **argument** but with a different meaning. The equivocator treats the different uses of the word or phrase as if they have the same meaning.

For instance, consider this variant of a well-known **deduction**:

All men are mortal.
Pelé is a man.
Yet Pelé is immortal.
So at least one man is immortal.

or this one:

All men are mortal.
Boudicca was not a man.
So it's possible that Boudicca is immortal.

In the first example how can it both be true that Pelé is a man (and so mortal) and that Pelé is immortal? This seems to be equivalent to saying that Pelé is mortal and that Pelé is not mortal: a bald **contradiction**. The answer is that the words 'mortal' and 'immortal' are being used in a confusing way that allows someone to be both without contradiction. 'Mortal' here means 'will die'; but 'immortal' does not refer to absence of bodily death, rather it refers to those whose fame will endure after they have died. When used in this way there is no contradiction in claiming both that a man will die and yet be immortal.

The second example provides a further example of equivocation. This time the word used in different senses is 'man': in the first premise, where it occurs in the plural, it is clearly intended to mean 'human beings'; in the second premise it is intended to mean 'male human being'. Both of these examples are somewhat far-fetched: they are deliberately paradoxical in their conclusions and unlikely to cause genuine confusion.

Consider another example, this time slightly more realistic. Someone might argue along these lines:

> It can never be right to deceive anyone deliberately.
> So no one has a right to deceive anyone deliberately.

The first premise uses the word 'right' to mean 'morally right'; the second seems to be referring to *legal* rights, which, although related, are not the same sort of thing. Clearly many actions which are morally wrong are not forbidden by the law: for instance, it might be morally wrong to eat meat which has been cruelly produced, but, as things stand, you have a legal right to do so if you please. Moving in this way from what is morally right, to what you have a legal right to do is a form of equivocation. This sort of equivocation typically arises from carelessness; however, many instance of equivocation involve wilful misunderstanding (see also **straw man**).

If, for example, someone advocates equality as a political goal, it is highly unlikely that they intend 'equality' to be understood as meaning 'total uniformity'. The demand for equality is typically a demand for equality of treatment, equality of respect, equality of access to power, equality of opportunity, the discounting of irrelevant features, and so on. It is almost never a demand that everyone be given precisely the same treatment in every respect. Nor is its aim to create a world in which everyone is as close to identical as possible. Yet some critics of egalitarianism oscillate between interpreting 'equality' in the ways described above, and as 'uniformity'. Their argument typically takes the following form:

> You want equality (of treatment, respect, access to power, opportunity, etc.).
> Equality (in the sense of complete uniformity) is an unachievable and undesirable goal.
> Therefore what you desire is unachievable and undesirable.

Stated in this way it is easy to see that this sort of criticism involves equivocation about the meaning of 'equality'. Such equivocation is not necessarily deliberate. When it *is* deliberate it is usually a form of **sophistry**, or, perhaps, **wishful thinking**.

etymological fallacy

The unreliable and often misleading move from a word's original meaning to its current meaning.

A form of the **genetic fallacy**, the etymological fallacy is an **informal fallacy**. Etymology is the study of the origin of words. This sort of move is sometimes informative, but is not at all reliable: because a word or phrase originally meant one thing, the **assumption** is that it will always keep that meaning, even when it forms only a part of a word and is used in a different context perhaps thousands of years later, often in ignorance of the original meaning. But etymological analysis is only *sometimes* of value in understanding contemporary meaning: it does not follow that because a word originally had one meaning that it will always continue to have that same meaning or even one directly related to it. Those who have spent many years perfecting their knowledge of ancient languages find the etymological fallacy extremely tempting and frequently succumb to it. Nevertheless etymology should only be used when it is genuinely illuminating. The trouble with it is that the meanings of words are not fixed entirely by their origins, though words often do preserve vestiges of their original meanings. The most reliable indicator of a word's meaning is its current use rather than its derivation (see also **dictionary definition** and **stipulative definition**).

For instance, the word 'posthumous' is composed of two Latin words, 'post' meaning 'after' and 'humous' (*humus*) meaning 'earth' with the implication of burial in earth. 'Posthumous' is currently used to refer to a child born after its father's death, or else, more commonly, to a book published after its author's death. So the essential meaning is 'after death'. However, someone committing the etymological fallacy might insist that 'posthumous' couldn't accurately be used to refer to the offspring or writing of someone whose body was lost at sea, or cremated, because they wouldn't have been buried in earth. This would be **pedantry**. It would also betray an ignorance of the nature of language.

The word 'drab' originally meant 'female prostitute'. However, if somebody today describes a woman's clothes as drab, this merely refers to her dress sense rather than her profession. The word 'horror' comes from a Latin word which suggests the bristling of hairs in fright: this etymological fact is interesting and does largely coincide with current usage inasmuch as, for instance, a horror movie is the kind of movie designed to make the hairs on the back of your neck bristle. But the etymological fact in no way fixes the meaning for all time.

The etymological fallacy is sometimes committed in political speeches as a form of **rhetoric**. Speech-writers often begin by looking up the origin of a key word in a speech. They then elaborate on this to make the points required by their commission, purporting to unpack interesting meanings latent in the word in question. So, for example, someone advocating more extensive cross-party debate of political questions in the British Parliament might draw attention to the fact that the word 'Parliament' comes originally from the French word *parlement* meaning 'talking', and then use this to argue that *therefore* (a case of the **spurious 'therefore'**) there should be more discussion of issues in Parliament (see **bad reasons fallacy**). However, the present meaning of 'Parliament' cannot be reduced to this; whether or not it retains a vestige of its original meaning, its central meaning is the supreme legislative body of the United Kingdom.

'everyone does it'

A familiar and inadequate excuse for bad behaviour based on the **companions in guilt move**. Usually this phrase should not be taken literally: 'everyone' doesn't mean *everyone*, rather it means 'many people' (see also **some/all confusion**). But just because many people do something that is wrong, it doesn't follow that it isn't really wrong.

So, for example, many people at some point in their lives drive through traffic signals just after they've turned red. If on a particular occasion you get caught by the police doing this, arguing that it isn't a serious offence because everyone else does it is a lame excuse. It *is* a serious offence because it can cause accidents. In this case it is fairly easy to see the inadequacy of the response: even if everyone actually did go through red lights on occasion this would not make it a less culpable offence, it would just make driving much more dangerous.

In other cases, such as pilfering stationery from work, many people use this excuse to themselves to make the action seem acceptable (see **rationalisation**). In this sort of situation saying 'everyone does it' amounts to saying that such theft is socially acceptable. However, just because something is socially acceptable it does not follow that it is morally acceptable (unless, of course, you believe that morality is nothing more than an encoded form of what is socially acceptable).

Politicians who, when asked about the apparent corruption within their party, deflect the question on to the fact that in many other countries such corruption is rife are avoiding the issue (see **irrelevance** and **politician's answer**); just because corruption is widespread it doesn't mean that it shouldn't be eradicated wherever possible.

Sometimes this sort of ploy is used as an attempt to excuse wrongdoing by picking out companions in guilt who are far more guilty than the person in question. For instance, a house burglar when arrested might point out that the amount of money he has stolen is negligible when compared with the expense account fiddling and tax evasion that goes on amongst business executives every day. However, just because other people are as bad as you or worse, it doesn't follow that you aren't really bad. What does follow is that someone who wants to single you out but is not prepared to single out others who are equally bad or worse is being inconsistent (see **consistency**).

In fact whenever anyone uses the phrase 'everyone does it' as an excuse for their behaviour you should be alerted to the possibility that they are using a bad argument to support immoral behaviour. It is sheer **wishful thinking** to suppose that other people's bad behaviour in some way legitimises your own.

evidence

See **anecdotal evidence**, **empirical** and '**research has shown that . . .**'.

exception that proves the rule

A singular **counterexample** which tests the truth of a **generalisation**. The word 'proves' in this common expression can lead to confusion. In this context it means 'tests out': it is an archaic meaning. Unfortunately, since the usual meaning of 'proves' is 'confirms', or 'demonstrates', some users of this expression take it to mean 'the existence of a counterexample *shows* that the generalisation is true.' A moment's thought should reveal the implausibility of this use of the expression: counterexamples undermine rather than confirm generalisations.

So, for example, the existence of a black-leafed plant would be an exception to the generalisation 'all plants have either green or red leaves'. It would provide a counterexample to the generalisation. In the appropriate sense of 'proves', this exception would 'prove' the rule that all plants have either green or red leaves by showing that this is a **false dichotomy**. It would test out the rule and show it to be wanting. However, a user of the phrase 'the exception that proves the rule', by a kind of principle of **truth by adage**, might assert that the case of the black-leafed plant only further confirmed the generalisation: it is 'the exception that proves the rule'. When set out like this such a conclusion seems absurd. Nevertheless some people do use this phrase in this confusing way.

Another interpretation of 'the exception that proves the rule' is to mean 'the fact that the exception in question is an exception shows that the rule holds in general'. So, for example, the spelling mnemonic 'i before e except after c' is apparently refuted by a number of counterexamples including, for instance, the fact that 'seize' is spelt as it is. Someone might then describe 'seize' as 'the exception that proves the rule'. But once again, a moment's thought should reveal that an exception can only weaken such a rule, and never strengthen it. Such counterexamples suggest the need for *ad hoc* **clauses** to make the rule strictly applicable.

excuses

See **'everyone does it'**, **'it never did me any harm'**, **rationalisation** and **wishful thinking**.

F

fallacy

See **formal fallacy**, **informal fallacy**, **'that's a fallacy'** and many other entries in this book.

false charge of fallacy

See **'that's a fallacy'**.

false dichotomy

A misleading account of the available alternatives (see also **alternative explanations**). A dichotomy is a division into two alternatives; for example all fish are either scaly or non-scaly. A false dichotomy occurs when someone sets up a dichotomy in such a way that it appears there are only two possible conclusions when in fact there are further alternatives not mentioned.

For instance, in most contexts the phrase 'if you're not for us you must be against us' is a false dichotomy, since it ignores a third possibility, that of being totally indifferent to the group in question, and also a fourth possibility: that you haven't yet made up your mind. Similarly, someone who says that you must either believe that God exists or else that God doesn't exist is setting up a false dichotomy since there is the well-known third option of the agnostic, who maintains that there is insufficient evidence on the basis of which to adopt a position on so momentous a question. And even this may be a false trichotomy since some philosophers have maintained that there is a further position that you can adopt, for which there is as yet no name, that of believing that the notion that God exists is itself completely meaningless and so can be neither true nor false nor unproven.

Someone arguing that people should attend to their own interests might say that if you don't always put your own interests first, the only alternative is to be a martyr, constantly sacrificing your own desires for the sake of other people. This would be a false dichotomy because there are in fact many more options than the two extremes given here. For example, you might decide to help other people when they are in great need, but in all other cases put your own interests first, thus avoiding the complete denial of your own desires while still showing some concern for others' interests.

False dichotomies can be set up accidentally or deliberately (perhaps this too is a false dichotomy). When accidental they result from an inaccurate assessment of the available positions; when deliberate they are a form of **sophistry**.

family resemblance term

A name coined by the philosopher Ludwig Wittgenstein for those words or concepts which cannot be defined in terms of **necessary and sufficient conditions**.

For example, Wittgenstein pointed out that you would search in vain to find the essential features of all games, those features which made games games and not something else. If you think of football, tennis, chess, solitaire, Olympic games, and so on, it is hard to find features which they all share and yet which will distinguish them from all other activities. This, Wittgenstein thought, was because there is no defining feature of a game, only a pattern of overlapping resemblances between the different things we call games. The name 'family resemblance term' comes from the fact that different related members of a family can be recognisably similar without all sharing one or more common traits. Similarly, games can all be recognisably games without all, for example, having rules, or being competitive. These are features shared by some, but not all games.

The notion of a family resemblance term is a useful counter to those who claim that the **Socratic fallacy** genuinely is a fallacy, because it shows how we can understand and use many concepts without being able to give precise definitions of them. It also suggests why those who have attempted to give a plausible definition of such concepts as 'art' or 'the good life' by listing necessary and sufficient conditions, have been unsuccessful: if these concepts are family resemblance concepts, then they will always resist being pinned down by that approach to definition.

formal fallacy

Any invalid form of **argument**, that is, one in which the **premises** can be true without the **conclusion** necessarily being true (see also *non sequitur*). Unlike valid arguments (see **validity**), formal fallacies are not truth-preserving: their structure does not guarantee a true conclusion from true premises. Even if the conclusion does turn out to be true, it will not have been reached by a reliable method.

An example of a formal fallacy is provided by the familiar move of the witch hunt. For instance, someone concerned with the prevalence of witches might argue as follows:

> All witches keep black cats.
> My neighbour keeps a black cat.
> So my neighbour must be a witch.

This is fallacious reasoning since the structure of the argument is invalid. It doesn't follow from the fact that the neighbour keeps a black cat that she is a witch, even if the first premise is true. Premise one doesn't tell us that all black-cat-keepers are witches; only that all witches keep black cats, which is not at all the same thing. For the conclusion to follow from the premises the first premise would have to state that all *and only* witches keep black cats, otherwise it leaves open the possibility that some people who keep black cats aren't witches, and thus the possibility that the arguer's neighbour is not a witch. Even though when spelt out in this way it is relatively easy to pinpoint what is wrong with this way of arguing, at first glance the reasoning in this fallacy can still be seductive. The term 'fallacy' is used in a looser sense to mean any faulty reasoning. (See **informal fallacy** and **'that's a fallacy'**.)

G

gambler's fallacy

The mistake of believing that in games of chance your odds of winning increase the more times you lose. Gamblers are particularly prone to believe that if they haven't won for a long time their chances of winning on the next bet are greatly increased. In many games of chance, such as roulette, this is sheer **wishful thinking**. In a simple game of tossing a coin, heads is just as likely to come up as tails, assuming the coin is unbiased. So if I tossed the coin a hundred times I would expect it to come up heads approximately fifty times. Similarly, in roulette a red number is just as likely to come up as a black number (although there is not quite a 50 per cent chance of each because there is a green zero on most roulette wheels). From this sort of fact the uncritical gambler will conclude that if there has been a long string of heads in coin-tossing, or else a long string of red numbers in roulette, then, by some supposed 'law of averages', it is very likely that a tails or a black number will come up next.

However, as neither coins nor roulette wheels have memories, there is no way they can recall the results of previous spins and adjust the result of the present game of chance accordingly. Consequently every time an unbiased coin is tossed there is the same 50 per cent chance of it coming up heads and this probability never changes no matter how many times in a row it happens to come up tails; every time an unbiased roulette wheel is spun there is precisely the same chance that the ball will land on a black.

Gamblers who tell themselves, 'I didn't win today, nor the day before, so my chances of winning tomorrow must have been greatly increased', are sadly mistaken. They have fallen for a version of this extremely widespread **informal fallacy**.

There are, of course, some games in which the chances of winning or losing vary: for instance, so-called Russian roulette. Someone takes a gun and puts a single bullet into the magazine leaving five blank spaces. If he or she holds the gun to his or her head and shoots there is a one in six chance of getting shot. Assuming the gun clicks automatically on to the next slot in the magazine, the next person will have a one in five chance of getting shot; the next, one in four; and so on until someone does actually get shot. If, however, the magazine is spun after each person pulls the trigger, then, as in conventional roulette, the odds do not change from play to play: there is always a one in six chance of getting shot until someone actually does get shot. The gambler's fallacy consists of mistaking cases of the latter type of game for the former, though usually the results of miscalculation are less serious than when playing Russian roulette.

generalisation

See **provincialism** and **rash generalisation**.

genetic fallacy

An **informal fallacy** of the form '*x* originated from *y*, therefore *x* must now have some features in common with *y*', though usually the reasoning is implied rather than baldly stated. This is not a reliable way of arguing since in many cases the only link between one thing and its descendant is the genetic connection; just because one thing emerged from another it does not follow that the thing that emerged shares any important feature with its origin.

It is easy to see what is wrong with this style of reasoning by considering extreme examples: chickens come from eggs, but it in no way follows that adult chickens will crack when dropped, nor that they are an essential ingredient in meringue; books are printed on bits of former trees, but it doesn't follow that they will benefit from watering and annual mulching.

The philosopher Friedrich Nietzsche is sometimes accused of committing this fallacy in his book, *On the Genealogy of Morality*. There he purported to show the origins of key moral concepts in resentment and self-hatred. His idea was that by showing the historical origin of such altruistic emotions he had undermined the exalted place accorded to them in Christian morality. However, even if he was correct about the origins of these concepts it certainly would not follow that they are less important today because of their original source.

Bishop Wilberforce used the genetic fallacy for rhetorical effect (see **rhetoric**) when arguing against Charles Darwin's theory of evolution. In a public debate with Thomas Huxley, a defender of Darwin's ideas, he enquired on which side Huxley traced descent from monkeys, his grandmother's or his grandfather's. The implication was that if Huxley was descended from monkeys, then one or both of his grandparents must have had prominent monkey-like features. This was presumably meant as a **refutation** by means of the **absurd consequences move**. However, it was misleading in at least two ways. First, it was a caricature of Darwin's views (see **straw man**), since Darwin claimed that human beings had ape-like creatures as immediate ancestors, not monkeys; he also claimed that the process of evolution was gradual, taking place over thousands of years rather than several generations. But the other, more basic, mistake was Wilberforce's **assumption** that whatever was descended from monkeys must be monkey-like. Whether it is or not depends entirely on the nature of the descent.

A common form of the genetic fallacy arises when people examine the origins of a word in order to determine its current meaning (see **etymological fallacy**). In this and all cases of the genetic fallacy, it may be true that there is some important link between the original and its descendant, but the mere genetic relation does not guarantee it.

getting personal

Attacking the character of the person with whom you are arguing rather than finding fault with his or her argument. This move is traditionally known as arguing *ad hominem* (from the Latin for 'to the person'). Getting personal is, in most cases, a technique of **rhetoric**, since discrediting the source of an **argument** usually leaves the argument itself intact.

For instance, if a politician argued that lowering the speed limit in built-up areas would reduce accidents involving children, and a journalist attacked this on the grounds that the politician had been fined for drunken driving and speeding on several occasions, this would be a case of getting personal. The question of whether or not the politician is a safe driver is irrelevant to the question of whether lowering the speed limit in built-up areas will reduce accidents. The politician's claim is best assessed by examining the evidence in support of the **conclusion**. The journalist deflected attention from the argument under consideration towards the alleged **hypocrisy** of the person who put the argument forward. But it is clear that hypocrites can put forward excellent arguments: many do.

Take another example. If a member of an appointments committee makes a very strong case for a particular applicant being given the job, and it is subsequently learnt that this applicant had been having an affair with him at the time, then this fact might be taken to undermine the case made to the appointments committee. The member of the appointments committee had a **vested interest** in seeing that particular candidate succeed. However, the nature of the personal relationship in no way destroys the force of the case. If good reasons were given for employing this person above other candidates, then they remain good reasons. What would probably be unfair in such a situation is that the other candidates would not have had such a motivated advocate working on their behalf. If there was **prejudice** in favour of this particular candidate then getting personal about the appointer's involvement would be appropriate.

Obviously if an argument involves our taking factual premises on trust, then it would be appropriate to point out that the arguer is a compulsive liar, if this is so. In this sort of case getting personal is focused on a relevant aspect of the arguer's character and so is an acceptable move to make. However, in most cases getting personal focuses on irrelevant aspects of character, thereby deflecting attention from the arguments given.

gobbledygook

See **jargon**, **pseudo-profundity** and **smokescreen**.

good company fallacy

See **bad company fallacy, kowtowing, truth by authority** and **universal expertise**.

H

humptydumptying

Giving private meanings to words in common use. This takes its name from Lewis Carroll's Humpty Dumpty in *Through the Looking-Glass*. When Alice asks Humpty Dumpty what he meant by 'glory', he replies 'I meant "there's a nice knock-down argument for you!"' Alice protests that this isn't the meaning of 'glory'. 'When *I* use a word,' Humpty Dumpty answers, in rather a scornful tone, 'it means just what I choose it to mean — neither more nor less.'

This is **stipulative definition** of quite a bizarre kind, but less conspicuous humptydumptying can lead to confusion and mis-understanding, particularly when there is no explicit stipulation of what a word is being taken to mean. For instance, if in a debate about poverty someone insists that there is no poverty in Britain, provided that this person realises the circumstances of the poorest people in the country, it would become clear that he or she was humptydumptying: using the word 'poverty' in a very unusual way.

Or, to take another example: when admirers describe a notoriously cruel gangland killer as 'a truly good man' this can only be humptydumptying. They have hijacked the words 'truly good man' and used them to mean something quite different from what they usually mean.

The term 'humptydumptying' should be reserved for extreme cases of stipulative definition and idiosyncratic uses of words in common use. To label someone's use of language humptydumptying is to condemn it as obfuscatory. Words have public meanings and to treat them as if they don't usually leads to confusion and **ambiguity** (but see also **jargon**).

hypocrisy

Advocating one thing, but doing another. Hypocrisy is the charge levelled at those who don't practise what they preach.

For instance, the vicar who stands in the pulpit every Sunday proclaiming the virtues of sexual fidelity but who is himself a serial seducer of married parishioners is guilty of hypocrisy, as is the anti-smoking campaigner who surreptitiously smokes twenty cigarettes a day, and the philosopher who chastises others for their alleged reasoning errors but is incapable of reasoning coherently on any issue.

What is wrong with hypocrisy is in part that it reveals the hypocrite's inconsistent beliefs (see **consistency**). Hypocrites' expressed views are at odds with the implicit beliefs demonstrated by their behaviour. Anyone who *really* believed what they preached wouldn't behave in a way so opposed to it. But hypocrites are particularly obnoxious because, unlike people who just unwittingly hold inconsistent beliefs, they typically tell other people how they ought to behave whilst exempting themselves from the general principles they are peddling.

Nevertheless, hypocrisy in no way proves the hypocrite's preaching false (see **bad company fallacy**). The charge of hypocrisy is a form of *ad hominem* argument (see also **getting personal**) and may well be an **irrelevance** when what we are interested in is the truth or importance of a principle rather than the character of the hypocrite. This doesn't, however, make hypocrites any more pleasant to deal with.

hypothesis

A statement to be confirmed or refuted by evidence or **counter-example**. A hypothesis differs from a mere **assertion** in that it is put forward with a view to its being verified or falsified.

For example, a psychologist might begin to research the effects of environment on choice of career by putting forward the hypothesis that choices of career are almost entirely determined by environmental rather than hereditary factors. However, this hypothesis might be undermined by examination of identical twins (who have identical genetic inheritance) who happen to have been separated at birth. If a significant proportion of such twins choose to enter the same profession as their twin, despite different environmental factors, then this might undermine the hypothesis, or suggest it needs refinement of some kind, perhaps by adding *ad hoc* **clauses**.

A police inspector trying to solve a murder might work on the basis of the hypothesis that the victim knew the identify of her assailant. The inspector would then interview the various friends and relatives of the victim in an attempt to see if the hypothesis was correct.

hypotheticals

See **no hypotheticals move**.

iff

Logicians' shorthand for 'if and only if'.

ignorance

See **proof by ignorance**.

ignoratio elenchi

Latin name for missing the point. See **irrelevance**.

implicit

See **assumption** and **enthymeme**.

imply/infer

Two words with precise but different meanings which are sometimes used as if they were interchangeable.

Premises *imply* a conclusion if the conclusion follows logically from them. Premises, however, never *infer* anything: only a person can infer something. So, for example, I might infer from the fact that you are a woman and that all women are mortal that you are mortal. The premises 'All women are mortal' and 'You are a woman' *imply* the conclusion; I *infer* the conclusion.

The tendency to use these terms as if they meant precisely the same thing is similar to the practice of using 'refute' and 'repudiate' interchangeably (see **refutation**).

inappropriate precision

Giving information or figures to a greater degree of apparent accuracy than suits the context. Advertisers and others often use the results of surveys to substantiate what they say about their products. Sometimes they make claims to a degree of accuracy that can neither be based reliably on evidence, nor is likely to make any sense to the critical reader.

So, for example, if a company selling washing powder claims that 95.45 per cent of British adults agree that this powder washes whiter than any other, then this level of precision is clearly inappropriate. It is inconceivable that all British adults were surveyed, so the result must be based on surveys. But surveys are only samples and not necessarily this accurate when scaled up to the whole population. At best the company should be claiming that over 95 per cent *of those asked* agreed that their powder washes whiter than any other. Even if the whole population had been surveyed, to have given the result to two decimal points would have been absurd. The effect is to imply a high degree of scientific precision in the research. Frequently, however, inappropriate precision is an attempt to mask the unscientific nature of a study.

This sort of pseudo-precision is usually a form of **rhetoric**. It is a way of trying to convince the reader or hearer of a particular conclusion and of the high level of scientific accuracy of the data used in support of it. Yet, for those sensitive to this tendency, it is likely to have the opposite effect.

inconsistency

See **companions in guilt move**, **consistency** and **hypocrisy**.

induction

A method of reasoning in which true premises provide good grounds for believing the conclusion, but not certainty that it is true. Typically induction involves the move from a number of **empirical** observations to a generalisation. The truth of the premises gives the conclusion a degree of probability, but this falls short of certainty. Induction is usually contrasted with **deduction**. A deductive argument with true premises (a **sound argument**) provides conclusive support for its conclusion: if the premises are true the conclusion must be true. This is not so with inductive arguments: if the premises are true, and the argument a good one, this at best makes it probable that the conclusion is true. A good inductive argument is one which gives a high degree of probability that its conclusion is true. With inductive arguments this probability always falls short of certainty. Inductive arguments can never be valid (see **validity**), at least not in the sense in which deductive arguments are valid. The quantity and kind of evidence required to support an inductive generalisation varies from context to context.

Imagine observing a large number of roses, all of them having a strong fragrance. You might then conclude on the basis of your experience that all roses have a strong fragrance. This would be an example of inductive reasoning. It relies on an argument from analogy (see **analogy, arguments from**): you are saying that because all observed roses are similar in one respect, all the roses that can ever be observed are likely to be similar in this respect too. Your inductive generalisation however, may turn out to be false. The accuracy of your observation of the roses you have encountered does not guarantee the truth of your conclusion about all roses. It only supports it, giving you good reason to believe it, until it is undermined by a **counterexample**. There are, as it happens, roses which don't have any fragrance detectable by the normal human nose. So the generalisation, despite the supporting evidence, turns out to be false.

This is not to denigrate induction as a form of reasoning. We have to rely on induction every day: all our expectations about the ways in which the future will resemble the past are based on it. We expect water to quench our thirst on the evidence that it has done so up until now. We confidently expect the sun to rise tomorrow because it has risen every day of our lives. Yet inductive arguments can never make their conclusions more than highly probable.

inference

See **imply/infer**.

informal fallacy

Any faulty or unreliable type of argument apart from a **formal fallacy**. Informal fallacies may be perfectly valid forms of argument in terms of their logical structure. There are many entries on informal fallacies in this book. For example, the **etymological fallacy** is not an invalid form of argument, rather it is a way of arguing based on the false premise that a word's meaning is always fixed by its original meaning, or by the original meaning of its constituent parts. Wherever I have labelled a type of argument a fallacy I have indicated whether it is a formal or an informal fallacy. I might have avoided lexical **ambiguity** by coining an alternative term for 'informal fallacy'; however, as many of the ways of arguing described in this book have well-established names this would have required substantial renaming, which might well have been more confusing than staying with the term 'fallacy'.

There is a colloquial use of 'fallacy' which is best avoided: as a synonym for 'something false'. Thus in the sentence, 'It is a fallacy that we can achieve full employment' the speaker is using the word in this sense: simply asserting that it isn't true that everyone can have a job. There is no particular structure or technique or pattern of reasoning being singled out as the alleged fallacy; rather the speaker is using the term to express strong disagreement with the opposing view. This sense of 'fallacy' is sometimes used as a form of **rhetoric**: by playing on the connotations of the word, a polemicist may deliberately attempt to persuade readers or listeners that the opposing view involves bad reasoning, whilst all that is really being expressed is disagreement (see also **equivocation** and **'that's a fallacy'**).

insults

See *ad hominem* **move** and **getting personal**.

invalidity

See **validity** and **formal fallacy**.

irrelevance

Shifting discussion away from the point at issue by bringing in matters which don't relate directly to it. When used as a ploy this can take the form of the **politician's answer**: a technique for avoiding giving straightforward replies to direct questions; or else it might be due to introducing **red herrings** or perhaps **getting personal** or introducing **anecdotal evidence** in an inappropriate context. More often it is simply due to lack of mental focus: the result of failing to appreciate precisely what is at issue.

For instance, in a discussion about whether or not music should be a compulsory subject taught in schools, a speaker might mention that her grandfather was a professional pianist. Unless some further argument is included, this fact, interesting as it might be, is completely irrelevant to the matter in debate. Perhaps in this case the point of mentioning the fact was that the pianist in question had not benefited from compulsory music teaching in schools, but nevertheless had acquired sufficient skill to become a professional musician. However, even if this were spelt out, it is still irrelevant unless the justification for making music compulsory in schools was supposed to be that this is the only way in which to produce skilled musicians, which it clearly isn't. This example involves introducing an irrelevant **premise**; in other cases the **conclusion** argued for may itself be irrelevant.

For example, in a debate about the fire precautions in sports arenas it would be irrelevant to introduce an argument which had as its conclusion that tickets for most sporting events are many times the price they were ten years ago even allowing for inflation. This conclusion fairly obviously misses the mark. However, in conversation or debate it can take some time before you realise that the conclusion for which someone is arguing is actually of no relevance to the matter under discussion.

'it never did me any harm'

A common and particularly irritating form of **rash generalisation** in which someone defends some unattractive practice on the grounds that they survived having the same thing done to them. The implicit argument goes like this:

> You say that such and such a practice should not be allowed because it is harmful.
> I had to suffer this practice, but haven't been noticeably harmed.
> Therefore you have insufficient grounds for condemning the practice.

For instance, if a father objects to his son being caned at school, the head teacher might reply that his worries are unfounded as he was himself caned at school and yet was not harmed by this. However, this form of argument, apart from relying on **anecdotal evidence** and generalising from a single case, mistakes the objection to the practice.

It is entirely consistent with caning in general causing serious psychological damage to a child's development that some instances of it leave some children entirely unscathed: the claim is not that every instance of caning necessarily causes serious harm. Rather, the usual objection to caning in schools is that in a large number of cases it can cause psychological damage and sometimes even serious physical damage. The fact that the head teacher was caned and remained apparently unharmed in no way justifies the practice. In extreme cases this style of arguing can be a crutch for morally disturbing **wishful thinking**.

This way of arguing may also involve wishful thinking of another kind: often the claim 'it never did me any harm' is simply false. People who frequently say 'it never did me any harm' are often seen to be protesting too much. The repeated insistence that they haven't been harmed is psychologically revealing in that it suggests the opposite: that they *have* been harmed, or else they wouldn't be so desperate to insist that they haven't. In some cases, it may be that the individual concerned feels that since they had to experience some hardship, then other people ought to suffer it too. So, for example, someone who endured two years of compulsory national military service might well use the 'it never did me any harm' move to try to persuade others of the value of military service in general when in fact what he or she she really means is, 'I had to suffer this, so I don't see why you shouldn't have to suffer it too.'

J

jargon

The specialist terminology associated with a particular profession or area of interest. The term 'jargon' is almost always used in a pejorative sense to suggest that language is unnecessarily obscure; 'technical term' is the label used for specialist words which are needed to communicate effectively about particular areas of specialism but which do not descend to the level of jargon. The same words can be jargon in one context and technical terms in another.

For example, most computer manuals are filled with jargon words such as, 'bytes', 'RAM disk' and 'hardware flow control template'. These words count as jargon because, in the context of an instruction manual aimed at the general reader, they are obscure; in a manual aimed at computer experts they would simply be technical language, and entirely appropriate. Computer manual writers still don't seem to recognise the difficulty most readers have with computer jargon.

Philosophers have their own portfolio of jargon which includes many Latin words and phrases such as *mutatis mutandis* (meaning 'making appropriate changes') and *prima facie* (meaning 'at first glance'); many of these have perfectly acceptable English equivalents. Some philosophers use philosophical jargon as a way of making their work seem more difficult and important than it really is (see **smokescreen**) since such writing requires initiation into the meaning of the jargon.

In closed groups of people communicating amongst themselves, such as university academics, jargon words take root very quickly. Unfortunately this tendency often puts the subject matter beyond anyone who hasn't been initiated into the meaning of the relevant jargon. (See also **newspeak**.)

K

knock-down argument

An **argument** which completely refutes a position (see **refutation**): the equivalent in argument of a knockout punch in boxing.

For instance, some people argue that all truths are relative to the culture in which they are expressed; on this view, it was true seven hundred years ago that the sun went round the earth (since that was then the official view), but is not true today. However there is a knock-down argument against this which demonstrates that it is a self-refuting position: if all truths are relative, then the theory that all truths are relative must itself be relative, that is, only true for some cultures. However, defenders of the theory of relativism usually treat it as if it were *absolutely* true. This knock-down argument at a blow refutes relativism, at least in its simplest form. Relativists, however, might treat this as an attack on a **straw man**, but then the onus would be on them to show how the argument caricatures their position.

knock-on effect

See **domino effect**.

kowtowing

Being overly deferential. There have been many great thinkers in history and it can be tempting to treat anything whatsoever said by a thinker whom you greatly admire as if it were obviously true. Sometimes there may be excellent reasons for relying on the opinions of experts and the authority of those who have devoted their lifetime to the study of a particular subject (but see **truth by authority** and **universal expertise**). However, this attitude can be taken too far and degenerate into obsequiousness and excessive humility, which gets in the way of critical thought. Kowtowing means, literally, touching the ground with one's forehead as a sign of deference.

For instance, even though Friedrich Nietzsche had many interesting and profound thoughts on a range of subjects, it would be merely kowtowing to him to take seriously his pronouncements on women (he famously declared, 'When thou goest to a woman take thy whip'), just because he is a thinker whom you respect. Uncritical acceptance of other people's ideas leads to mental stagnation.

L

lawyer's answer

Responding to direct questions in a way that is factually accurate yet misleading – usually deliberately misleading. Not as blatant as **lying**, giving this sort of response, like being **economical with the truth**, can be morally equivalent to a lie since its intended and actual effect is almost indistinguishable from that caused by a lie. I have labelled it the 'lawyer's answer' as this is a technique that some lawyers use when questioned on sensitive topics. Many legal decisions turn on technicalities and strict interpretations of wording. Consequently lawyers are often highly skilled at using phrases in their answers that do not incriminate them or their clients; yet at the same time, they answer, or at least seem to answer, the questions asked. Obviously not all lawyers use this diversionary technique, and not all the people who use it are lawyers (see **some/all confusion**). It is a device public figures who don't want to be shown to be liars often use.

For example, former President of the United States Bill Clinton declared in response to aggressive questioning about his relationship with Monica Lewinsky, the intern with whom he was believed to have had an affair, 'I did not have sexual relations with that woman, Ms Lewinsky'. The truth of this statement depended on the meaning given to the phrase 'sexual relations'. As it later emerged, Clinton had had oral sex with Lewinsky and had also left semen stains on one of her dresses. Their relations may, however, have stopped short of full penetrative sexual intercourse. On one reading Clinton was deliberately deceiving those questioning him as he knew they would understand 'sexual relations' as meaning 'any sexual interaction'. Yet at the same time he avoided an outright lie – something that could have had more serious legal consequences for him – because he understood 'sexual relations' to be synonymous with 'full sexual intercourse'.

For those who believe that an outright lie is more pernicious than a truthful yet deliberately misleading statement, giving a lawyer's answer may be an attractive option in a difficult situation. In many cases it is easier to prove an outright lie than it is a deception of this kind.

leading questions

See **complex questions**.

least worst option

A choice that may not be attractive, but is the best of those available. Representative democracy has famously been labelled 'the least worst option' amongst forms of political organisation. It has a number of points in its favour, including, for example, allowing political leaders to be deposed by a majority of voters; but it also has features that count against it, such as voters may be swayed by factors that are not relevant to a candidate's ability to be a good political leader. But if you accept that there is no better way available of organising society, it is 'the least worst option'. Calling it the 'best' option would give it a more positive connotation because it seems to imply that it is unequivocally good.

There are many situations in which we have to make a choice between alternatives, when none stands out as a good choice. In such situations, assuming that we really do have to make the choice, it is rational to choose whichever we believe to be the best of the alternatives, while recognising that the choice we make falls short of being ideal. As a parent, we may have a choice of only three schools our children can attend locally, none of which fits with our ideal of what a school should be like. We must make a choice and take the least worst option, while recognising that our choice does not vindicate the local council for giving us such a poor choice of schools, or endorse the particular school as excellent (it may be mediocre or worse).

The novel *Sophie's Choice* by William Styron centres on a terrible choice a mother must make between saving one of her two children, a boy and a girl; or letting them both be killed by Nazis. She takes what she sees in that instant to be the least worst option, that of saving her son who, she tells herself, will have a better chance of survival. But this agonising choice inevitably haunts her.

Recognising that what we have done in a situation is to have chosen the least worst option rather than endorsed everything about our choice is important. We should be clear about the limitations of alternatives available to us, and the degree to which our decisions are governed by pragmatic considerations in most real life situations.

lexical ambiguity

See **ambiguity**.

lexical definitions

Another term for **dictionary definitions**.

loaded questions

See **complex questions**.

lying

Writing or saying something which you know or believe to be untrue. Lying is almost universally condemned but very widely practised.

Some people believe that lying is absolutely wrong and can never be justified whatever beneficial consequences might ensue. Typically they derive this view from religious beliefs. Others think that lying is wrong because it frequently has harmful consequences. Even if it doesn't have any harmful effects in a particular case, it is still morally wrong because, if discovered, lying undermines the general practice of truth-telling on which human communication relies. For instance, if I were to lie about my age on grounds of vanity, and my lying were discovered, even though no serious harm would have been done directly, I would have undermined your trust generally so that you would be far less likely to believe anything I said in the future. Thus all lying, when discovered, has indirect harmful effects. However, very occasionally, these harmful effects might possibly be outweighed by the benefits which arise from a lie. For example, if someone is seriously ill, lying to them about their life expectancy might conceivably give them a chance of living longer, whereas telling them the truth could possibly induce a depression that would accelerate their physical decline. In such cases, lying might be the lesser of two evils, though the decision whether or not to lie would be an unenviable one to have to take. (See also **economy with the truth**.)

M

majority vote

See **democratic fallacy** and **truth by consensus**.

many questions

Another name for **complex questions**.

missing the point

See **irrelevance**.

modus ponens

Latin name for **affirming the antecedent** (see also **antecedent**, **consequent**, **denying the antecedent**, **affirming the consequent**, **denying the consequent**).

modus tollens

Latin name for **denying the consequent** (see also **antecedent**, **consequent**, **affirming the antecedent**, **affirming the consequent**, **denying the antecedent**).

N

necessary and sufficient conditions

A necessary condition is one which is a prerequisite; as, for example, being able to read is a necessary condition of your making sense of this book. This isn't a sufficient condition, because you might be able to read, yet still find the book too abstract for you to make sense of it. Being able to read doesn't guarantee that you'll be able to make sense of it, but if you can't read, you certainly won't make any sense of it. A sufficient condition is one which if met will guarantee that whatever is in question will be satisfied; as, for example, it is a sufficient condition for working legally in the United States that you possess a Green Card. (This is not a necessary condition, because US citizens don't need a Green Card to work legally; in other words, being a US citizen is another sufficient condition of working legally in the United States.)

Some philosophers have argued that a necessary condition for something being a work of art is that it is an artifact; this can't be a sufficient condition for being a work of art since numerous artifacts quite clearly aren't works of art, my garden shed, for instance. Some philosophers have maintained that being placed in an art gallery and appreciated for aesthetic qualities is a sufficient condition for something being a work of art: anything that is treated in this way, on this account, must be a work of art. (See also **family resemblance term** and **Socratic fallacy**.)

newspeak

The name George Orwell gave to the language created by the rulers in his dystopian novel *Nineteen Eighty-Four*. The language was supposed to control thought, making some ideas simply impossible to think.

For instance, the word 'sexcrime' was used to cover all instances of sexual intercourse (apart from procreation between man and wife, which was known as 'goodsex'). By lumping all other forms of sexual activity together under the heading 'sexcrime', the language was supposed to limit the possibility of thinking about non-procreative sex in any detail. This approach to language involves the controversial **assumption** that language shapes our thought to the extent that if you have no word for something you cannot think about it.

The word 'newspeak' is sometimes used as if it just meant **jargon**, as in 'I can't bear all this computer newspeak'. However, this use is misleading; newspeak is far more sinister than jargon since it supposedly makes some thoughts unthinkable (rather than just impenetrable).

no hypotheticals move

A rhetorical technique (see **rhetoric**) used to avoid answering awkward questions about what might happen. A hypothetical situation is one which might conceivably occur. So, for example, one hypothetical situation we might well find ourselves in is that the world's oceans and rivers become so polluted that it is no longer safe to eat fish caught in the wild. This is not actually the case now, but it could be the case in the future. Most planning for the future involves envisaging hypothetical situations and deciding how we might deal with them if faced with them in reality. Military training, for example, is based on anticipation of what might happen; a sports coach will usually run through a series of hypothetical situations before a big game in order to help players work out how they should react; civil engineers building a dam will base their calculations on informed hypotheses about projected rainfall and the likely water level; and so on.

However, some people in positions of authority have devised a way of avoiding commitment to particular courses of action. Whenever they are asked a question about what they would do in some hypothetical situation they respond that that is irrelevant and that they needn't answer questions about what *might* happen: they have to deal with the real world, not an imaginary one. In other words, they refuse to answer the question solely on the grounds that it is about a hypothetical situation. This is simply a rhetorical trick: the no hypotheticals move. Obviously some questions about far-fetched hypothetical situations don't merit an answer (but even some of these do: see **thought experiments**).

For example, if someone asked 'What would you do if you discovered that the entire British Royal family were members of the Sicilian mafia?', very few people would see any point in venturing an opinion; the question is simply too far-fetched. But the question 'What will be the implications for the British constitution if the monarchy is abolished?' is a much more realistic one and certainly deserves an answer because it deals with a possible situation. The answer to it is of great interest, and no doubt could affect those who are in a position to set in motion a chain of events which could culminate in the abolition of the monarchy. Dismissing the question as merely hypothetical and therefore not worth answering would be a straightforward case of avoiding an important issue.

Politicians, who are particularly prone to use the no hypotheticals move, should bear in mind that all policy statements express views about how a party will behave in a range of hypothetical situations (typically, for example, beginning with the hypothetical situation in which the party in question is elected to power). If they are prepared to deal with hypothetical situations in the context of policy-making then they need to have some further grounds for dismissing hypotheticals beyond the mere fact that hypotheticals deal with what might happen rather than what has actually happened (see **consistency** and **companions in guilt move**).

non-contradiction, principle of

See **contradiction**.

non sequitur

A statement which does not follow logically from the **premises** which precede it. The phrase is Latin for 'it does not follow', but it is commonly used in English and there is no obvious English equivalent. *Non sequiturs* are most obvious when absurd. For instance, from the facts that most cats like milk and some cats have tails I could not derive the conclusion that David Hume was the greatest British philosopher. That would be a complete *non sequitur* that borders on the surreal, whether or not its conclusion is true. *Non sequiturs* are often advertised by the spurious use of 'so' and 'therefore' (see **spurious 'therefore' and spurious 'so'**), but the context of a statement can also suggest that it is a conclusion derived from what has gone before even when there is no such word used to indicate it.

Any **formal fallacy** will have a *non sequitur* as its **conclusion**, though most of these *non sequiturs* will be less obvious than the one given above. Formal fallacies are by definition invalid forms of argument (see **validity**), which is just another way of saying that their conclusions do not follow from their premises.

Some statements may look like *non sequiturs* at first glance, but on closer inspection will turn out to follow from unstated **assumptions**. It might, for instance, seem that someone who said 'this meal contains meat so you shouldn't eat it' was guilty of drawing a conclusion that did not follow from the given premise, since the conclusion 'you should not eat it' does not follow from the fact that it contains meat. However, the speaker may here quite reasonably have been assuming the unstated premise 'you are a vegetarian'. Given this tacitly understood context, the conclusion is not a *non sequitur* at all but rather the conclusion of an **enthymeme**, an argument with a suppressed premise. Real discussion is peppered with such apparent *non sequiturs*. On closer examination many of these will turn out to be conclusions drawn from shared assumptions. Nevertheless, genuine *non sequiturs* are common too; some of these stem from carelessness, others from **wishful thinking**.

O

obscurantism

See **jargon** and **pseudo-profundity**.

Ockham's razor

A principle of simplicity. If you can explain something adequately without introducing further complexity, then the simple explanation is the best explanation. This principle, sometimes known as the principle of parsimony, is named after the medieval philosopher William of Ockham. It is often given in the form 'Don't multiply entities beyond necessity', though this is not how Ockham himself expressed it. What Ockham's razor means in practice is best shown through an example.

Scientists trying to discover whether or not the Loch Ness monster exists might examine supposed photographic evidence. If the evidence can plausibly be explained as the result of known causes, such as otters swimming, or sticks floating in the water, then the scientists would be well-advised to apply Ockham's razor and refrain from hypothesising the existence of a unique monster to explain the evidence. There is no need to go beyond the known range of phenomena to explain the photographic evidence. No further entities need be invoked to explain the traces on the film.

In general applying Ockham's razor is an excellent idea. However, the most obvious practical problem comes in deciding what counts as a simple explanation and what as a simplification. As in so many areas of critical thinking sensitivity to context is vital.

oversimplification

See **black-and-white thinking** and **straw man**.

P

paradox

An unacceptable conclusion derived by seemingly unassailable reasoning from apparently uncontroversial **premises**. 'Paradox' is a precise term in philosophy; in ordinary conversation 'paradoxical' is often used as a synonym for 'odd' or 'unexpected'. The philosophical use is narrower than this. Genuine paradoxes draw attention to inconsistencies in beliefs or anomalies in reasoning. They are often more than logical puzzles and have in many cases forced philosophers to revise their unquestioned **assumptions**.

An example of a paradox is the famous case known as the heap or sorites paradox ('*soros*' is Greek for heap). If 5,000 grains of salt make a heap, then taking away a single grain will still leave a heap. So with taking away a further grain. And another one. And another one. And so on. But if we apply this reasoning, in 4,999 steps we will be left with a single grain, which clearly isn't a heap. Presumably the heap ceased being a heap some time before getting down to the single grain. But when did this happen? Working back the other way: a single grain of salt isn't a heap; nor are two grains; nor three. So when do we get a heap? The paradox here is that if either removing or adding a grain of salt cannot cause something to become or cease to be a heap, it seems to follow that a single grain of salt must be a heap, since we can reduce any heap of salt to a single grain by a series of uncontroversial stages of removing single grains. Yet we know very well that a single grain of salt is not a heap.

One half-serious solution to this paradox is to point out that one grain can't be a heap. Nor can two or three: they can only make a triangle or a pillar of salt. But, since four grains can make a pyramid, then this is the point at which a collection of grains can become a heap. Neat as this solution is, it doesn't provide a solution to the many other instantiations of this paradox: the example of the heap is just an example. There are many other similarly vague terms (see **vagueness** and **drawing a line**), such as 'tall' and 'bald' for which there is no sharp boundary between possessing and not possessing this attribute. Reducing a tall woman's height by a millimetre isn't going to stop her being tall; plucking a single hair from a man's head isn't going to suddenly make him bald (unless you use 'bald' in an extremely precise sense to mean not having a single hair on one's head, rather than the vaguer way in which it is usually used).

In general we should reserve the word 'paradoxical' to describe genuine paradoxes rather than for merely odd or unusual circumstances. Otherwise we risk a loss in precision. (For discussion of other colloquial uses of precise terms see **begging the question, Catch-22** and **validity**.)

parsimony, principle of

See **Ockham's razor**.

pedantry

A niggling and inappropriate concern with detail, often at the expense of what is really important in an issue. 'Pedantry' is always used in a pejorative way.

For example, a pedant reading this book might complain that the first sentence of this and many other entries has no main verb and so is not strictly speaking a grammatically correct sentence. Yet if I had struggled to recast the definitions of terms as grammatically correct sentences I would have had to sacrifice clarity and conciseness, both of which are more central to my aims than grammatical correctness. What's more, the decision to begin each entry in this way was a conscious one, not an accidental transgression of some law of grammar; to focus on this aspect of the book at the expense of the content would be mere pedantry and as such completely inappropriate. Slavish rule-following, particularly in the realm of grammar and syntax, is a typical mark of the pedant: this is not to say that we should abandon all rules, only that most grammatical rules should be broken where strict adherence to them would undermine the aims of the writing.

A pedantic park keeper might decide to change all the park signs from 'Please do not walk on the grass' to 'Please keep off the grass' on the grounds that the first set of signs did not explicitly exclude dancing, hopping, crawling and running on the grass. This sort of pedantry about possible ambiguities of phrasing (here the alleged **ambiguity** is over the precise meaning of 'do not walk') is typical of the pedant: most pedants are insensitive to the context of utterances and so see possible confusions where none are likely.

The charge of pedantry can be used as a form of **rhetoric**. Those intent on persuading others of their position may simply dismiss any criticism as pedantry. If you find fault with the detail of someone's reasoning or evidence you may unfairly be accused of being a pedant. In fact, this accusation is often made against people who are rigorous in their critical thinking. The most effective way of meeting it is to demonstrate that attention to detail in the particular case is appropriate and relevant. Unfortunately there is no easy rule for discriminating between pedantry and an appropriate and commendable attention to detail. What is required is a sensitivity to the standards of scrutiny appropriate to the particular context.

personal attacks

See *ad hominem* **move** and **getting personal**.

persuader words

Words such as 'surely', 'obviously' and 'clearly' whose main role is to persuade the reader or listener of the truth of what is being asserted. They are used for rhetorical effect (see **rhetoric**).

In many cases the use of such words is justified because it would be tedious to trot out the overwhelming evidence in support of a particular assertion prefixed by, for example 'obviously'. Life is too short to waste time defending every one of our **assertions**, particularly when there is a very good chance that the person we are addressing will share many of our beliefs about the matter. However, there are times when something more is needed than the rhetorical flourish of using a few persuader words. In some cases persuader words are used to smuggle in unwarranted conclusions. Off-guard listeners or readers might find themselves nodding in agreement at these familiar trigger words without stopping to consider whether or not what is being asserted is *obviously* true. If someone says 'Obviously we should believe any testimony given by the police', the word 'obviously' is standing in for an argument to this conclusion whilst at the same time inviting us to agree with the speaker. But what is the **premise** implied by this word? Presumably it is something like 'The police would never falsify evidence or lie under oath.' However, this suggested premise is a false one: unfortunately there are cases when police officers have falsified evidence and lied under oath. The use of the persuader word rather than the premise makes it easy for a listener to avoid considering what is really at stake. This sort of use of persuader words is not always conscious, particularly in conversation. Users of such words are not always trying to persuade you of something which they know to be untrue; often they are simply using a shorthand way of expressing their own beliefs.

persuasive definition

A form of **rhetoric** in which a word is defined in a particularly **emotive** or question-begging way (see **begging the question**). Typically the definition will then be used to reach the desired conclusion on the matter under discussion.

For instance, someone who defined 'democracy' as 'mob rule' would be guilty of using a persuasive definition since the connotations of the word 'mob' are negative and no doubt calculated to arouse opposition to democracy; in most discussion about democracy this sort of definition would beg the question about the value of democracy.

petitio principii

Latin name for **begging the question**.

pettiness

See **pedantry**.

poisoning the well

Indirectly denigrating a position by pre-emptively ridiculing, discrediting or insulting its source. This is a very common form of **rhetoric**. One way of poisoning the well is to begin a sentence with 'No one could possibly believe that . . .', or 'Only a fool would argue that . . .' or 'Some naïve people believe . . .' or a similar phrase.

Here's a specific example. Imagine a speaker who declares:

'Only a racist would be opposed to large-scale immigration to Britain'

By pre-emptively labelling anyone opposed to large-scale immigration a racist, the speaker here leaves very little room for his or her opponent to manoeuvre without appearing to be a racist. Put in this way, this is a mere **assertion**. Argument in support of the position is needed; otherwise it is simply a technique for making those with whom the speaker disagrees afraid to make their point.

Poisoning the well makes it very difficult for anyone to respond by endorsing the view that has been poisoned in this way. It also insults anyone who holds a different opinion. Add to this that most people prefacing their statements with such phrases know very well that the people they are addressing are inclined to endorse the discredited view, and you can see that this is a devious move in argument. Once you have recognised and named this kind of rhetoric it is fairly easy to identify particular instances of it. The best way to confront it is with a straightforward denial of the poisonous element of the statement, followed by an explanation of why your position is a reasonable one to hold. You might also consider challenging the speaker to explain why they believe that 'only a racist' would argue for this position, pointing out that this is an unsubstantiated assertion and may even be a case of **begging the question**.

politician's answer

A kind of **irrelevance** which is often encountered when politicians are interviewed on radio or television. It is a rhetorical technique (see **rhetoric**) by which they avoid giving direct answers to questions which they don't really want to answer in public. Instead of giving a direct answer to a direct question, the politician delivers a short (or sometimes quite long) speech on a related topic. The trick is to make the speech internally coherent; thus the politician seems to give a confident and plausible performance in response to what should be probing questions. This diversionary tactic allows him or her to avoid giving an honest response to a potentially damaging question and also provides air time for a short party political broadcast. It is a kind of **economy with the truth**.

For instance, a politician asked, 'Do you intend to put up taxes while you are in office?' — a simple direct question inviting the response 'yes' or 'no' — might well reply by discussing the opposing party's policy on taxation, or the virtues of a particular style of taxation, or perhaps the virtues of his or her own party's past approach to taxation: in other words by avoiding the specific question asked. Unless you are listening closely, it can be easy to forget what the initial question was and be carried along by a flow of rhetoric. Unfortunately this technique is not confined to politicians (from whom we have come to expect devious face-saving rhetorical techniques) but is used by many other people in responsible positions who want to avoid facing up to their responsibilities. (See also **red herrings**.)

post hoc ergo propter hoc

Latin for 'After this therefore because of this', or to spell it out more fully, 'whatever happened after this must have happened because of this': a kind of **correlation = cause confusion**.

prejudice

A belief held without good reason or consideration of the evidence for or against its being true. 'Prejudice' is sometimes used in a wider sense than this to mean any obnoxious view whether or not its holder has examined the evidence in support of it; however, this use of the term dilutes its meaning.

For example, a judge who knew that the defendant had previously attacked a policeman might not listen impartially when the same person came before her accused of the same sort of attack. She might already have decided that the accused was guilty. An employer might be prejudiced in favour of a candidate for a job simply because they both went to the same college even though this is not a relevant criterion for performing the job in question. In other words the employer would already have made up her mind that the candidate was the best suited for the post before examining any relevant evidence. A landlord might be prejudiced against all students on the grounds that one student tenant once left without paying his rent. In this case, as with many cases of racial and sexual prejudice, a whole group of people are treated as if they shared common characteristics, when it is clear that there is no great homogeneity within that group (see **rash generalisation**).

Critical thinking is opposed to prejudice. We are all riddled with prejudices on a wide range of issues, but it is possible to eliminate some of them by making an effort to examine evidence and arguments on both sides of any question. Human reason is fallible, and most of us are strongly motivated to cling on to *some* beliefs even in the teeth of evidence against them (see **wishful thinking**); however, even making small inroads into prejudice can transform the world for the better.

premises

Suppositions from which **conclusions** are derived. Premises are the parts of an **argument** which give reason for believing that the conclusion is true or false.

For example, in the following argument two premises lead to a conclusion:

Premise one: If you travel on a transatlantic flight you will arrive at your destination tired.
Premise two: You are travelling on a transatlantic flight.
Conclusion: Therefore you will arrive at your destination tired.

Notice that even if neither of the premises is true, the argument is still a valid one (see **validity**); however, if the premises are true then the conclusion must be true.

presupposition

See **assumption** and **supposition**.

principle of non-contradiction

See **contradiction**.

proof by ignorance

An **informal fallacy** in which lack of known evidence against a belief is taken as an indication that it is true. However, ignorance of evidence against a position does not prove that there could not be evidence against it; at best it is only indirect support for it.

For example, no one has provided conclusive evidence that watching violence on television causes children to be more violent than they would otherwise be. There are so many variables that have to be controlled for in order to establish this causal connection that this is hardly surprising (see also **correlation = cause confusion**). To conclude from this lack of proof that *therefore* violence on television *doesn't* cause children to become more violent than they would otherwise be is a mistake. It is easy to see why this won't do, since precisely the same lack of evidence could be used to 'prove' the opposite case: that *therefore* violence on television *does* cause children to become more violent than they would otherwise be. Both conclusions are ***non sequiturs***.

Although no one has provided conclusive evidence that there is no life after death it would be extremely rash to treat this as a conclusive proof that there is. By the same technique we could prove that everyone will be damned to eternal torture after death, or that we will all be reincarnated as stick insects.

Part of the temptation to believe that proof by ignorance is real proof may stem from the fact that in some courts of law a defendant is presumed innocent until proven guilty. In other words, lack of evidence against someone is taken as proof, for the purposes of the court, that they did not commit the crime. However, as many cases of guilty people being freed because of lack evidence show, this isn't really a *proof* of innocence, but merely a practical, if imprecise, way of protecting innocent people from wrongful conviction.

provincialism

Generalising about the right way to behave on the basis of how people behave in your locale is sometimes known as provincialism (see also **rash generalisation**). It is an unreliable way of arguing. The name itself embodies **prejudices** about people who live in the provinces: the idea is that they do not travel and have relatively little knowledge of the ways of the world and so have a tendency to assume that what they do in their particular locale should hold for the rest of the world, or at least is the best way of going about things: clearly not safe generalisations to make on the basis of available evidence.

So, for example, because on high table in an Oxford college antiquated table manners dictate that you should peel a banana with a knife and fork, some dons may believe that people who peel bananas with their bare hands lack refinement.

pseudo-profundity

Uttering statements which appear deep but which are not. One of the easiest ways of generating pseudo-profound statements is to speak or write in seeming paradoxes (see **paradox**). For instance, if you say any of the following in a serious manner some people will probably think you are saying something particularly important about the human condition:

> Knowledge is just another kind of ignorance.
> Moving leaves you in precisely the same place.
> The path to true virtue is through vice.
> Shallowness is an important kind of depth.

Whilst meditation on some of these statements may reveal interesting possible interpretations, and in an appropriate context they might indeed be profound, once you have appreciated how easy they are to generate you will be less likely to be taken in by them.

Another way of achieving pseudo-profundity is to repeat banal statements as if they were profound, a technique favoured by some popular psychologists:

> At birth we are all children.
> Adults aren't always nice to each other.

A third way of generating pseudo-profundity is to ask strings of **rhetorical questions** and to leave them hanging in the air without attempting to provide answers to them:

Are humans ever truly happy?
Is life a meaningless game?
Can we ever know ourselves?
Does everyone suffer from self-doubt?

Profundity arises from answering these questions, not just from asking them.

Q

question-begging

See **begging the question**.

questions

See **complex questions** and **rhetorical questions**.

quibbling

See **pedantry**.

R

rash generalisation

A general statement based on insufficient evidence (see also **anecdotal evidence** and **provincialism**).

For instance, if, on the basis of a conversation with one taxi driver I were to conclude that all taxi drivers are anti-racist I would be guilty of a rash generalisation. Even if my sample of taxi drivers consisted of all the taxi drivers working for a particular taxi company, then to conclude that *all* taxi drivers are anti-racist would clearly be going far beyond the evidence. I would need to know that my sample was a representative one, and have reasons for supposing that there was something about being a taxi driver that predisposed people to being anti-racist, or at least that there was a one-to-one correlation between these two things. What's more, I would probably have to ignore a number of **counterexamples** which would certainly undermine the conclusion; if I encountered only one racist taxi driver in my life, this single case would be sufficient to undermine a generalisation of this kind.

It would be rash to generalise from the fact that a single British athlete at the Olympic Games was found guilty of taking banned performance-enhancing drugs that all or most of the British Olympic team are similarly guilty. Unless there were a plausible explanation of why this generalisation might hold, such as that an athletics coach was putting pressure on all athletes to take these drugs, it would clearly be going far beyond the evidence to maintain the conclusion.

rationalisation

Disguising the real reasons for acting in a particular way by giving a self-serving justification which, even if plausible, is not true (see also **wishful thinking**). In extreme cases, rationalisers come to believe their own rationalisations.

For instance, someone might rationalise their picking up and keeping a gold watch found in the street, as: 'Well, I know it's wrong, but if I hadn't done it someone else would have done. And besides, if I took it to the police no one would bother to collect it, so it would be a waste of everyone's time and energy' (see also **'everyone does it'**). It is transparent to most observers in such a situation that the real motivation for holding on to the watch is that they want to keep it, but the rationalisation of the action makes it seem more socially acceptable. (See also **'it never did me any harm'**.)

A government might rationalise its active support for one side in a civil war in a distant country, claiming that it was intervening on humanitarian grounds when in fact the overarching reason was to maintain access to that country's rich mineral reserves.

red herrings

A form of **irrelevance** which leads the unwary off on a false trail. A red herring is literally a dried fish which when dragged across a fox's trail leads the hounds off on the wrong scent. Deliberate introduction of irrelevant topics into a discussion is a frequently used ploy. It is particularly effective because it may not be obvious for some time that the trail is a false one, since, typically, red herrings have intrinsic interest and seem at first to be pertinent to the question under discussion. They are particularly damaging to debate when time to discuss the issue is limited (see **politician's answer**).

For example, if in a debate about freedom of speech someone began to describe the structure and functioning of the Internet this might at first seem to have some relevance to the issue. But if no connection were made back to issues of freedom of speech sooner or later you would realise that the speaker had gone off at a tangent and introduced a topic which, although interesting in itself, did not, as used, have anything directly to do with the topic under discussion.

reductio ad absurdum

A phrase used to refer to two related moves in argument. The primary meaning of the phrase is a technical one in logic whereby you prove the truth of a particular statement by supposing for the sake of the argument (see **supposition**) that it is false, and show that this supposition leads to a **contradiction**. As this technique is rarely if ever employed in everyday argument there is little point in giving a contrived example to illustrate it.

The second, far commoner, and far more useful technique which goes under the name of *reductio ad absurdum* is that of refuting a position by showing that it would lead to absurd consequences if true. For instance, if someone claimed that all differential treatment on grounds of sex is morally wrong then I might point out that this would lead to the conclusion that having separate changing rooms for men and women at the swimming pool is morally wrong, since no women are admitted into the men's changing room, and no men into the women's. Yet, intuitively, this is an absurd belief. So we can confidently reject the claim that *all* differential treatment on grounds of sex is morally wrong. (For further examples, see **absurd consequences move**.)

referential ambiguity

See **ambiguity**.

refutation

Proof that a statement, allegation, or charge is untrue. This should not be confused with repudiation: if you *repudiate* a statement you simply deny that it is true. For instance, it is simple to refute the **assertion** that no one ever grew rich from writing books about philosophy by citing a single **counterexample**, such as Jostein Gaarder, the author of *Sophie's World*. Repudiation does not require evidence or argument; refutation, on the other hand, does. Unfortunately many people use the word 'refute' as if it were interchangeable with 'repudiate'. Often, for instance, politicians will claim to have 'refuted' an opponent's point when all they have done is deny that it is true. The temptation to use the word 'refute' in this way may stem from **wishful thinking**: it might just be that it's nice to think that you've undermined an opponent's position simply by denying it. However, in the precise sense of these terms, refutation usually requires considerably more effort than repudiation.

refutation by counterexample

See **counterexample**.

repudiation

See **refutation**.

'research has shown that . . .'

A phrase often used to persuade the listener that the speaker can back up what he or she is saying with firm **empirical** evidence. However, it is extremely vague (see **vagueness**) to claim that 'research has shown' anything unless you can back up the claim with specific details about the alleged research. Who carried out this research? What methods did they use? What precisely did they find? Have their results been confirmed by other workers in the field? These are the sorts of questions which anyone who uses this phrase should be able to answer.

If they can't, then there is no reason to be persuaded by the phrase, which is then empty of content.

Indeed, people who are experts in a particular area are very unlikely to use a phrase as vague as 'research has shown that'; they are far more likely to mention specific research. So this phrase should put you on your guard. Some people who use this phrase may sincerely believe that research has shown what they believe it to have shown. But more often than not this is simply **wishful thinking**. If it turns out that research has indeed shown what they claim it to have shown, this is usually a lucky coincidence rather than something the speaker really knew. (See **bad reasons fallacy**.)

rhetoric

The art of persuasion. Rather than giving reasons and presenting **arguments** to support **conclusions**, those who use rhetoric employ a battery of techniques, such as using emphatic **assertion**, **persuader words** and **emotive language**, to convince the listener or reader that what they say or imply is true.

For instance, one rhetorical technique favoured by charities advertising in newspapers is to set up a **false dichotomy**: 'You can either send £50 to our charity, or you can ignore the suffering of others.' This sort of dichotomy suggests that there are only two options, one of which is unattractive; thus you should be persuaded to give money to the charity. In fact there are many other things that you can do that demonstrate that you are concerned about others' suffering.

Another technique favoured by advertisers is to use visual rhetoric to persuade you that their product is one you should buy by linking it with a glamorous lifestyle; the implication is that if you buy the product then you too will have a glamorous lifestyle. If you had good reasons to believe that, say, buying a particular type of car would catapult you into a world of beautiful people, then this wouldn't be merely rhetoric; there would be reasons for your belief. However, in most advertising of this kind, there is no plausible case made to this effect, and in many cases when the implicit argument is spelt out it is obviously absurd. Nevertheless, the psychological effect of seeing a particular product associated with glamour can be very strong.

There is nothing intrinsically wrong with using rhetoric, and it has its place in the kind of speech that is aimed at changing people's opinions. However, frequently rhetorical flourishes mask weak evidence and faulty reasoning.

rhetorical questions

Questions which are asked purely for effect rather than as requests for answers. Sometimes the questioner assumes that there is only one possible answer to the question, in which case the rhetorical question functions in precisely the same way as **persuader words**. In this form rhetorical questions are simply substitutes for straightforward statements: 'Who could doubt that . . .?' and 'Would anyone want to live in a world in which . . .?' are in most uses equivalent to 'No one could doubt that . . .' and 'No one would want to live in a world in which . . .' Whether or not you use such questions is largely a matter of personal writing or speaking style.

However there is another form of rhetorical question which is sometimes used to avoid providing a clear position on the point at issue. For instance, a writer investigating the topic of free will might end a paragraph with, 'And are we really free to choose anyway?' Such a rhetorical flourish is perfectly acceptable if the writer is prepared to answer the question. But if it is left hanging there it is a form of intellectual laziness.

It is comparatively easy and certainly unhelpful to raise a large number of seemingly deep questions on almost any topic (see also **pseudo-profundity**); what is difficult and important is finding answers to them.

ridicule

See *ad hominem* **move**, **getting personal** and **straw man**.

S

sayings

See **truth by adage**.

sentimentality

Inappropriate emotion. The person who is absolutely overwhelmed with sugary joy at the cuteness of a kitten, or who idealises a lover, is guilty of sentimentality, emotion that is inappropriate or completely disproportionate to the situation. A sentimental person is one who is prone to such exaggerated and often gushing responses to the world, and typically uses this as a strategy of avoidance, a way of refusing to confront unpleasant truths (such as that the kitten has worms and would quite happily disembowel a live mouse on the rug, or that the lover has bad breath).

Sentimentality is a fault, not a virtue. It is an obstacle to critical thinking, since it is a way of avoiding unpleasant truths. It is a common psychological block to clarity of thought that often involves **wishful thinking** in that the sentimental person is unwilling to confront facts and is much happier in a soft cuddly world of their own imagination. Sentimentality can even involve blindness to the way things really are. It can be a kind of magical thinking that involves reacting to the way the individual would like the world to be rather than to the way it is. Oscar Wilde famously declared a sentimental person one 'who desires to have the luxury of an emotion without paying for it'.

For example, the mother of a child who has been caught bullying another child may simply refuse to believe that her son could be a bully. In her eyes he remains this sweet innocent child who could never harm anyone else, and she experiences nothing but warm and comforting feelings in his presence. How could he possibly be the culprit? There must be some mistake. These bruises and cuts must have another cause. This is a sentimental reaction, a way of avoiding the unpalatable truth that her son is a vicious bully.

self-deception

See **wishful thinking**.

shifting the goalposts

Changing what is being argued for in mid-debate. This is a very common move to avoid criticism: as soon as an arguer sees a position becoming untenable, he or she shifts the point of the discussion on to a related but more easily defended one.

So, for example, if I began by defending the claim that all killers without exception should automatically receive a sentence of life imprisonment, you might point out that within the category of 'killer' there is a wide range of people, some of whom cannot be held fully responsible for their actions on grounds of mental illness. If I then continued as if I had all along been arguing only about murderers who had been fully responsible for their actions, I would have subtly shifted the goalposts whilst not acknowledging a change in what was being argued for.

Often the move of shifting the goalposts is made easier by a certain **vagueness** about what was being argued for in the first place. (See also **irrelevance** and **zig-zagging**.)

single case, arguing from

See **anecdotal evidence** and **rash generalisation**.

slippery slope argument

A type of **argument** which relies on the **premise** that if you make a small move in a particular direction it may then be extremely difficult or even impossible to prevent a much more substantial move in the same direction (see also **domino effect**). If you take one step down a slippery slope you run the risk of finding yourself sliding downwards at an ever-increasing speed until you reach the bottom. The further down the slope you get the harder it is to stop. After a while you can't stop even if you desperately want to. This metaphor of a slippery slope is often used either explicitly or implicitly as a way of persuading people that the acceptance of one relatively innocuous practice will inevitably lead to the legitimation of highly undesirable practices.

For instance, using this style of argument, some people maintain that euthanasia should never be legalised in any form because that would involve taking the first step down a slippery slope which has at its bottom morally abhorrent practices such as murder and even genocide. You shouldn't take the first step unless you are prepared to descend rapidly towards this highly undesirable end point, it is alleged. In this particular case the argument is usually bolstered by appeal to a frightening precedent: the fact that some of the Nazi techniques of mass murder were first piloted as what was described as a form of euthanasia. The slippery slope argument suggests that were we to make any form of deliberate killing legal now we would very likely find ourselves moving helplessly down a steep slope towards the legalisation of less acceptable forms of killing until we ended up sanctioning murder and worse.

This form of argument can have some force, but in order to judge it we need extensive information about the alleged inevitability of the descent; it is not enough simply to claim that there is a slippery slope. Typically, slippery slope arguments obscure the fact that in most cases we can decide how far down a slope we want to go: we can dig our heels in at a certain point and say 'here and no further'. And we can have very good reasons for this (see also **drawing a line**). The metaphor of slipperiness with its connotations of inevitable descent and frightening loss of control does not seem to allow this possibility. It conjures up images of powerlessness which may be inappropriate to the case in question. Sometimes slippery slope arguments are pure **rhetoric** designed to obscure the fact that the descent towards the worst possible scenario is by no means inevitable.

In its most extreme forms this kind of rhetoric can easily be ridiculed. Using the same sort of move it would seem to follow that if we eat at all we are in serious danger of eating more and more until we end up obese; if we tell a small white lie we will end up by betraying our country; if we permit a surgeon to perform minor operations without using anaesthetics we will be well on the way down a slippery slope which will end with the legalisation of human vivisection without anaesthetic. And so on. What these exaggerated examples demonstrate is that much more information about the kind of slope is needed before we can say that it is so slippery that the end result of the first step will be disaster. Slopes have different degrees of slipperiness and in most cases there are straightforward ways of avoiding the descent to the bottom. Even if actual slopes are hard to negotiate, the sort encountered in slippery slope arguments usually allow us to dig our heels in before we lose control.

The slippery slopes discussed so far all rely on **empirical** questions about the alleged inevitability of descent. Some slippery slope arguments also rely on a logical point about how if one small move in a particular direction is justified then any number of such small moves must also be justified (see **drawing a line**).

A different metaphor sometimes used as an alternative to the slippery slope is that of the thin end of the wedge. Once a wedge has been inserted in a crack it can usually be pushed further and further in until the thicker end has prised open the crack. Here the thick end of the wedge represents an undesirable end point. The metaphor of the slope suggests loss of control; that of the wedge an irresistible force. In both cases the sense of inevitability created may be inappropriate to the case in question, and the use of such metaphors should alert you to the possibility that you are being persuaded by rhetoric rather than argument.

It is worth noting that the term 'slippery slope' is almost always used by critics of an argument rather than by its defenders, and that it can itself be a rhetorical device used to caricature an opponent's argument (see **straw man**).

smokescreen

A rhetorical trick (see **rhetoric**) in which an arguer disguises his or her ignorance or deviousness behind a screen of meaningless **jargon**, **pseudo-profundity** or **sophistry**. At first glance the unwary listener is likely to be taken in by the intelligent-sounding pronouncements; on closer inspection it turns out that nothing of any importance has been said.

so

See **persuader words** and **spurious 'therefore' and spurious 'so'**.

Socratic fallacy

The mistaken belief that if you can't define a general term precisely you won't be in any position to identify particular instances of it. This **informal fallacy** gets its name from Socrates the great Athenian philosopher, who has been accused – probably falsely – of implicitly endorsing this mistaken **assumption**. Socrates' method, at least as it is portrayed in his pupil Plato's dialogues, was to demonstrate the limits of his contemporaries' understanding of central concepts, such as 'virtue' or 'justice', by getting them to attempt to define these terms and then providing a range of **counterexamples** and difficulties for their definitions.

Although this fallacy, like many fallacies, has a superficial plausibility, on closer inspection it becomes clear that lack of a precise definition does not necessarily stop us from using a concept effectively in most instances. For example, those who fall for this fallacy might claim that unless you can give a completely watertight definition of 'off side' in soccer, you won't be able to identify particular instances of a player being off side. Yet it should be obvious that very few footballers and football fans would find it easy to give a precise definition of 'off side', yet are very skilled at recognising whether or not a player actually is off side. Or, to take another example, most of us feel confident to declare certain individuals beautiful despite being unable to give a precise definition of 'beauty'.

It is clear that being able to give precise definitions of some concepts may on occasion be extremely useful in deciding whether or not borderline cases fall within the concept. However, we are usually able to recognise what something is without being able to give a very precise definition of the concept within which it falls. This may be because the type of concept defies definition in terms of **necessary and sufficient conditions**: it might be what the philosopher Ludwig Wittgenstein dubbed a '**family resemblance term**'. For example, Wittgenstein thought that 'game' was a family resemblance term: there is no common defining essence of all games, merely a pattern of overlapping and criss-crossing resemblances between the things which merit the label game. If he was right about this, any attempt to define 'game' using the conventional method of stating necessary and sufficient conditions would be futile.

some/all confusion

A kind of **ambiguity** that arises when the words 'some' or 'all' are omitted and the context does not make it absolutely clear which is intended.

For example, the sentence 'Cats have tails' could be understood in several different ways. It could mean '*All* cats have tails', in which case it is false since Manx cats don't. It could mean '*Most* cats have tails', which is true. Or it could mean 'Cats *typically* have tails', which is also true.

In most cases the context eliminates ambiguity. However, this is not always so. One reason for needing to know which meaning is intended is that a statement beginning 'All' such as 'All footballers are fit' can be refuted by a single **counterexample**; whereas statements such as 'Some footballers are fit', 'Most footballers are fit' and 'Footballers are typically fit' cannot so easily be refuted (see **refutation**).

Sometimes people leave out the words 'some' or 'all' in order to make their pronouncements appear stronger than they really are. For instance, someone might say:

> Women are physically weaker than men.
> You are a woman.
> So you must be physically weaker than me because I'm a man.

This is a kind of **sophistry**. The first **premise** can only plausibly be taken to mean 'Most women are physically weaker than most men' or 'Women are generally weaker than men'; it certainly can't mean '*All* women are physically weaker than *all* men', which is fairly obviously false. Yet that is precisely how the arguer has taken it. Only if it is taken in this way does the **conclusion** follow from the premises: otherwise it is a *non sequitur*.

sophistry

A display of cleverness which doesn't respect the principles of good reasoning but smuggles in unlikely conclusions under a cloak of sham argument. It is a catch-all term for a whole range of dubious techniques including **begging the question**, **circular arguments**, **equivocation**, **formal and informal fallacies**, **pseudo-profundity**, and **rhetoric**.

For instance, the following is sophistry:

Sophist: This cat is your mother.
Cat owner: That's ridiculous: how can this cat be my mother?
Sophist: Well, you're not denying that this cat is yours are you?
Cat owner: Certainly not.
Sophist: And isn't it true that this cat is a mother?
Cat owner: Yes.
Sophist: So this cat must be your mother.
Cat owner: Oh.

In this case it is relatively simple to see that the sophist's conclusion is false, and not much more difficult to see why it doesn't follow from the established premises. However, in more complex chains of reasoning the sophistry may be more artfully disguised and more pernicious in its effects.

The sophists were ancient Greek teachers who allegedly taught their pupils how to win arguments by any means available; they were supposedly more interested in teaching ways of getting on in the world than ways of finding out the truth. Whether or not the real sophists were as unscrupulous as they have been made out to be, the modern use of the term 'sophistry' is always pejorative and usually suggests that the arguer is a charlatan who is well aware of the shortcomings of his or her arguments.

sorites paradox

See **black-and-white thinking, drawing a line**, **paradox**.

sound argument

A valid argument (see **validity**) with true **premises** and so a true **conclusion**. For example, the following is a sound argument:

All human beings are members of the species *Homo sapiens*.
I am a human being.

So I am a member of the species *Homo sapiens*.

However, the next example, despite being valid, is not sound:

> All kangaroos are insects.
> Skippy is a kangaroo.
> So Skippy is an insect.

spurious 'therefore' and spurious 'so'

An inappropriate use of the word 'therefore' or 'so' to persuade listeners or readers that something has been proved when in fact it hasn't. The words 'therefore' and 'so' are usually used to indicate that what follows is the **conclusion** of an **argument**, either explicitly stated or implied. For instance, in the following argument, the word 'therefore' is used correctly to indicate that what follows is a conclusion derived from the given **premises** by means of **deduction**:

> All fish live in water.
> Socrates is a fish.
> Therefore Socrates lives in water.

The word 'so' could equally well have been used in place of 'therefore'. In everyday speech it is often tedious and unnecessary to spell out all the premises of an argument, since it is usually reasonable to assume that the person with whom we are talking shares many of our **assumptions**. We would probably be inclined to say something like: 'Socrates is a fish, so of course he lives in water', rather than give the full argument as above. This is an **enthymeme**, an argument with a suppressed premise (that all fish live in water). There is nothing wrong with this provided that it is clear what has been left out.

However, some writers and speakers exploit the persuasive power of 'therefore' and 'so', and liberally sprinkle their prose with these words, even though they do not offer any argument for their would-be conclusions. This is an easy alternative to arguing for your conclusions and many casual readers are taken in by it. But in fact the supposed conclusions which follow spurious uses of 'therefore' and 'so' are *non sequiturs*. For instance, if someone says 'Boxing often causes brain damage, so it should be banned', the conclusion which follows 'so' could have been derived from several different suppressed premises, such as 'Any activity which often causes brain damage should be banned' or 'Sports which often cause brain damage should be banned' or 'If boxing often causes brain damage then it should be banned'. This list does not exhaust the possible alternatives. But unless the premise is obvious in the context, or else actually stated, the use of 'so' is spurious: it gives the superficial appearance of an argument, but in fact is merely a disguised **assertion**. It is either a case of sloppy thinking, or else an attempt to persuade by means of a rhetorical device (see **rhetoric**).

stipulative definitions

Definitions which are the result of conscious and explicit decisions about how a word or phrase is to be used, rather than definitions based on the analysis of how words are usually used (see **dictionary definitions**). Giving a stipulative definition of a word or phrase is tantamount to saying, 'This is how I shall use this word or phrase even if it is sometimes used with a slightly different meaning.' To avoid confusion it is often necessary to make clear precisely what you mean by a particular word or phrase. This is especially important if you are using it in an unusual way or when it has a number of possible interpretations. Usually this means giving a narrower or at least more selective definition than is found in the dictionary. It would be absurd to stop to give definitions of all the important terms in an **argument**. In order to communicate at all we need to make many **assumptions** about shared linguistic knowledge and beliefs. However, particularly in the realm of **empirical** research, stipulative definitions of key terms can prevent confusion.

For instance, a team of psychologists conducting research in education might stipulate that when they describe someone as 'intelligent' what they mean, for the purposes of the research project, is that this person is capable of scoring more than 100 on an IQ test.

The word 'intelligence' is somewhat vague unless given a precise definition or used in a context where one is implied. Giving a stipulative definition here avoids confusion by making explicit how these researchers are using the term.

However, sometimes use of stipulative definitions can lead to misunderstandings. If someone were to read the psychologists' report in the above example forgetting that the word 'intelligent' was being used in this way, they would, quite reasonably, understand the term in a more colloquial sense. The result would be a failure of communication. Such misunderstandings are most likely to occur when stipulative definitions are given for words which are in common use and when the stipulated definitions differ significantly from the everyday ones.

It is important to realise that words in common use are difficult to rid of their typical associations and that many readers will quickly revert to the more common use of a term unless frequently reminded of the stipulated definition. 'Poverty', for instance, is a highly **emotive** word suggesting extreme want and lack of basic necessities such as food, shelter and clothing. Some sociologists, however, use the term in a different way, stipulating that poverty is always relative to the typical social needs of a particular society. Using this stipulated definition it may turn out that someone in contemporary Britain who cannot afford to own a colour television set is for this reason to be considered to be in a state of poverty. Yet when the results of this sort of sociological investigation into poverty are published in daily newspapers, most readers find it difficult to keep in mind the special definition of 'poverty' being used. Words are stubborn: they resist having their everyday meaning wrenched from them, and in many cases it is better to coin a new term than to stipulate an unusual meaning for an old one (see also **humptydumptying**).

straw man

A caricature of your opponent's view set up simply so that you can knock it down. Literally a straw man is a dummy made of straw used for target practice. Setting up a straw man in argument is the opposite of playing **devil's advocate**. Sometimes it is a deliberate ploy; in which case it is a disreputable form of **rhetoric**. More often it involves a degree of **wishful thinking** stemming from widespread reluctance to attribute great intelligence or subtlety to someone with whom you strongly disagree. Over-confidence in your own position may lead you to treat dissenting views as easy targets when in fact they may be more complex and resistant to simple attacks.

For example, in a discussion about the merits and demerits of zoos someone might argue that zoos can serve an important conservation role for endangered species. An opponent of zoos might misrepresent this point, perhaps by treating it as equivalent to the view that only endangered species should be kept in zoos. One way of doing this would be by suggesting that the defender of zoos' view was absurd because it would imply that we should liberate non-endangered zoo animals. Clearly the defender of zoos was only giving one possible defence of zoos, rather than suggesting that it was the only defence of them. So by misrepresenting the defender's position, the arguer sets it up as an easy target to knock down.

Dr Johnson made a famous attack on Bishop Berkeley's philosophy of idealism (which claimed that we can't be sure of the continuing existence of unperceived physical objects except on the hypothesis that God continues to perceive them) by kicking a large stone and declaring, 'I refute it *thus*.' His point was that it was impossible to believe that something so solid was really just composed of ideas: but Johnson was mistaken if he really thought that Berkeley's idealism would not be able to explain the fact that Johnson's toe hit solid rock. Only a caricature of Berkeley's views would be vulnerable to such a point. So Johnson had set up a straw man. Whilst it is often tempting to set up and topple easy targets this activity has no place in critical thinking.

subject/motive shift

See **getting personal**.

sufficient conditions

See **necessary and sufficient conditions**.

sunk cost fallacy

The self-destructive tendency to carry on investing in a failing project, idea, or enterprise on the grounds that you have already invested heavily in it. This involves **wishful thinking**.

For example, if you have bought a television that keeps breaking down and you have paid many hundreds of pounds to have it repaired, you may be tempted to keep fixing it on the grounds that you have already invested this money in it. This is probably foolish. You might, on environmental grounds, be concerned about throwing out a television set that could be repaired, but if your reason for keeping it is solely that you have already invested in it by having it repaired again and again, then you have fallen for the sunk cost **fallacy**. Just because you have invested large sums of money in it, it doesn't follow that the best course of action is to keep channelling funds in this direction. You need therapy that will make you let go of that investment and realise that, to quote a saying, you are simply 'throwing good money after bad' (but see **truth by adage**).

Politicians in wartime may be unwilling to withdraw troops from combat on the grounds that this would mean that soldiers who have already been killed in the conflict would have given their lives in vain. This may be a further example of the sunk cost fallacy. The cost of the dead soldiers' lives was high, but this in itself would not provide adequate justification for risking more soldiers' lives. The issue should be focused on what resolution there could be to the conflict, not on the high investment in human life already committed to it.

supposition

A **premise** assumed (see **assumption**) for the sake of argument but not necessarily believed; sometimes known as a presupposition.

Suppositions, unlike **assertions**, are not presumed to be true; rather they are instrumental in finding out what is true.

For example, a police inspector might say the following, 'Let's suppose the murderer did enter the house by the window. Surely then we'd expect to find some evidence of a forced entry.' The inspector is not asserting that the murderer definitely did enter the house by the window; nor even that that is probably what happened. The inspector is inviting us to follow through a chain of reasoning based on the supposition that the murderer came in through the window. In other words the inspector is offering a hypothesis about what might have happened.

In a debate about video nasties someone might ask, 'Suppose that you are right that watching video nasties triggers violence in a small percentage of viewers. Can we be sure that they wouldn't have found other triggers if video nasties didn't exist?' Here the speaker probably doesn't even believe that watching video nasties does trigger violence, but shows that even if it could be shown that such videos can trigger violence it doesn't follow that they are unique in this respect. In other words, the speaker is asking you to suppose for the sake of argument that watching video nasties can trigger violence. (See also **devil's advocate**.)

suppressed premises

See **assumptions** and **enthymeme**.

sweeping statement

See **rash generalisation**.

sycophancy

See **kowtowing**, **truth by authority** and **universal expertise**.

syntactical ambiguity

See **ambiguity**.

T

technical terms

See **jargon**.

'that's a fallacy'

The manoeuvre of falsely accusing someone of committing a fallacy
(see **formal fallacy** and **informal fallacy**). It is a form of **rhetoric**
which can be particularly pernicious. If you are putting forward a case
and someone confidently declares that what you have just said involves
a number of fallacies, then you may be tempted to back down, giving
your attacker the benefit of the doubt. But the onus should be on those
who accuse others of fallacious reasoning to spell out precisely why
they believe this to be a fair charge, otherwise the charge is at best
vague (see **vagueness**). The situation is made more complicated
because of the **ambiguity** of the word 'fallacy'; it can mean invalid
reasoning, an unreliable pattern of argument, or, in some contexts it

may simply be shorthand for 'I disagree with your last statement'. This latter use, like the increasingly common use of '**begging the question**' to mean 'suggests the question', should be avoided as it muddies the important distinction between a statement being thought false and a form of argument being fallacious.

The best defence against a claim that you have used a fallacy is to request an explanation of the charge from anyone who makes it.

'that's a value judgement'

A statement sometimes mistakenly treated by its utterer as a **knock-down argument** against what has just been said. The assumption so obviously being made by those who use this phrase to silence debate is that, for some usually unspecified reason, value judgements are not permitted in rational argument.

So, for example, in a debate about which authors' work should be included in the school curriculum one teacher might say 'The reason why we include *King Lear* on the curriculum is that it is a great play'. The response 'That's a value judgement' may then be heard. But the person using the words 'great play' undoubtedly realises that he or she is making a value judgement: that is the point of the statement. If the responder's implicit view is that it is a mistaken value judgment, then the onus is on him or her to provide evidence to back up this claim. Simply declaring that a judgement has been made in no way refutes the particular judgement, nor in most cases does it rule it out of court. Similarly, the person who declares *King Lear* 'a great play' needs to provide some evidence to support this view.

The idea that we should not make value judgements is not an easy position to defend in any context since almost every aspect of our lives which we are likely to argue about is infused with values: we make implicit value judgements in nearly everything we say. There is rarely any justification for deeming value judgements impermissible. The statement 'that's a value judgement' can itself be construed as a value judgement: it is a judgement that what has just been said is worthless because it makes a value judgement. The act of deeming worthless itself involves a value judgement, so this position is self-refuting.

therefore

See **persuader words** and **spurious 'therefore' and spurious 'so'**.

thin edge of the wedge

See **slippery slope argument**.

thought experiment

An imaginary situation, often far-fetched, intended to clarify a particular issue.

For example, in order to bring out what it is that we value about our lives, the philosopher Robert Nozick concocted the following thought experiment. Imagine that it is possible to plug yourself into an experience machine, a type of virtual reality machine which gives you the illusion of actually living your life but with the added twist that everything that you do or happens to you is intensely pleasurable. Whatever pleases you in real life can be simulated in its most pleasurable form in the experience machine; once you are plugged into it you will believe that all these pleasurable events are really taking place. Would you willingly plug into such a machine for the rest of your life? If, as in most cases, the answer is no, this suggests that you value some things more than just unlimited pleasurable experience, though you may not have realised this until you conducted the thought experiment.

The thought experiment of the experience machine is obviously far-fetched; it is very unlikely that such a machine will exist in our lifetimes. But that doesn't matter. The point of it is to pick out our fundamental attitude to pleasure, and it is good at making clear our intuitions on this. Consequently, to dismiss it simply because it is far-fetched is to miss its point. The real issue is not whether we would voluntarily plug ourselves into an experience machine, it is whether we really do value pleasure above all other things in life. The thought experiment gives us a way of testing our intuitions on this matter. (See also **conditional statements** and **no hypotheticals move**.)

truth by adage

The mistake of relying on familiar sayings as an alternative to thinking.

Many adages contain germs of truth, and some are indeed profound, but they aren't reliable founts of knowledge and can be misleading. For example, take the saying 'You can't teach an old dog new tricks'. This isn't true of all dogs, and certainly isn't true of all human beings (see **some/all confusion**): there are many older people who are capable of making radical leaps in their ability. This is not to deny the effects of ageing. The point is that what is roughly true, that as we get older it becomes harder to learn new behaviour, is not true for everyone in every respect. At most the saying captures the idea that it *may* be difficult to change the ways of an older person. However the saying implies that you can never teach any older person anything new, which is a **rash generalisation** and one which is fairly obviously false.

When such apparently wise sayings take on the role of authorities (see **truth by authority**) there is little space for critical thought. The appearance of profundity is not the same as genuine depth and you should be on your guard against people who readily resort to adage rather than to argument. Citing a familiar adage is rarely a satisfactory alternative to thinking about the particular case in question. Yet so often adages are spouted as if they necessarily embodied the wisdom of the ages in a way that should put an end to all discussion. Anyone using an adage should at least be able to demonstrate that it genuinely applies to the issue under discussion.

truth by authority

Taking statements to be true simply because an alleged authority on the matter has said that they are true. There are very good reasons for deferring to experts on a wide range of matters. Life is too short, and intellectual ability too varied for everyone to be an expert on everything. There is a division of intellectual labour which makes it sensible to seek the views of experts when we move into a realm in which we have little reason to feel confident about our own knowledge and opinions.

For instance, if I break a bone in my leg, although I have some vague notions of the best way to treat it, I would surely do better to seek expert medical advice from a doctor who has experience of the different kinds of fractures and has had the benefit of years of study of medicine than to rely on my uninformed hunches about the nature of my ailment. The doctor would be able to determine whether I have in fact broken my leg, or just bruised it badly; whether it is most likely to set correctly if put into plaster, or whether it should simply be rested, and so on. However, it isn't simply because the doctor claims to be an authority on fractures that what he or she says about my case is likely to be true; it is because the doctor reaches a conclusion on the basis of sound reasoning and medical knowledge, reasoning and knowledge which other doctors would be in a position to assess and, possibly, contest. Because I don't have the relevant medical knowledge I have to rely on the authority of the doctor's diagnosis, just as when I need legal advice I rely on a lawyer's assessment of the situation because I don't have a detailed enough knowledge of the law to be confident in my own judgements on the matter.

In such cases we seek out experts who have had the relevant training and whose performance is monitored by a professional body; that is why we feel confident to rely on their judgement. However, even in these cases a level of scepticism may be appropriate. Doctors and lawyers do not always agree, and where you suspect that the expert's opinion may be based on false **premises**, faulty reasoning or **vested interests** it is as well to seek a second opinion.

In some other cases, deference to experts may be entirely inappropriate (see **kowtowing**). One particularly dangerous psychological tendency that many people have is to put confidence in the views of authorities even when they are speaking on topics outside their area of specialisation. For instance, a Nobel-prize-winning physicist might be taken seriously by some when he or she speaks on the decline of morality (see **universal expertise**). Deference to experts is also inappropriate when seeking the truth on controversial issues where there is no consensus among the experts. For instance on many such questions in politics and philosophy it would be ridiculous to cite the authority of a famous political theorist or philosopher who has held the view you want to endorse if your aim is to provide evidence for the truth of that view. In controversies there will be numerous authorities which could be cited to disprove any particular side. Some philosophers seem to think that it is sufficient to show that Ludwig Wittgenstein (a famous twentieth-century philosopher) endorsed a particular view to prove that that view is true. But from the fact that Wittgenstein believed that something was true we cannot simply conclude that therefore it must be true (see **spurious 'therefore' and spurious 'so'**). In order to assess the truth of what he claimed it would be necessary to examine his reasons for claiming it and to examine the views which other philosophers have put up against him. Citing the authority of a philosopher is unlike citing the authority of a medical expert since in philosophy, unlike in medicine, most views are strongly contested.

The principal difficulty for someone faced with an expert's opinion is to decide how much weight to give it. The main points to bear in mind are that even if you establish that someone really is an expert in the field, he or she is still fallible; that experts often disagree with each other, particularly in areas where the evidence is inconclusive; and that, as mentioned above, experts are usually only experts in a relatively narrow area and so their pronouncements on areas outside their expertise should not be taken as seriously as those they make on their areas of expertise.

truth by consensus

Taking statements to be true simply because they are generally agreed upon. This is not a reliable way of discovering the truth on most issues;

just because there is general agreement that something is true it doesn't follow that it *is* true.

For instance, in the fourteenth century there was general consensus that the world was flat, but it doesn't follow from the fact that most people thought it was flat that it actually *was* flat. Only an extreme relativist about truth would want to maintain that. If the experts of the day believe something to be the case, this may make it likely that what they believe is true, or approaches the truth (see **truth by authority**). However, it is not the fact that they believe it that makes it true, rather the truth of their belief depends on whether or not it matches up with the way the world is. Even if experts in a particular field happen to agree about something it doesn't follow that what they agree about must be true, though if you are not an expert it would be appropriate to treat the consensus view of experts very seriously. But when the people in agreement aren't experts, and some of them know very little about the matter in question, there is no good reason for treating their consensus as an indicator of truth.

One reason why consensus isn't a reliable indicator of truth is that people are often very gullible: they are easily misled about all kinds of things, as any confidence trickster knows. What's more, most of us are prone to **wishful thinking** of various kinds. We believe what we wish were true, even if this doesn't match up to the facts, and sometimes even in the face of overwhelming evidence against our cherished beliefs.

Where there is no consensus, an even less reliable method of determining the truth is to rely simply on majority opinion. On most important questions the majority of people are ill-informed on what is at stake; it is surely better to rely on a minority of experts who have had time to study the available data rather than the hastily-formed views of the majority. For instance, it may be that the majority of the world's population today believe that our destiny is completely determined by astrological considerations. But most of the people who believe this have such a sketchy knowledge of astronomy that their views are of little significance in determining whether or not the positions of stars determine our behaviour. Consequently when someone begins a sentence, 'It is generally agreed that' or 'Most people believe that' you should determine precisely what work is meant to be done by this phrase. Why does it matter what is generally agreed? Are we supposed to conclude that because most people believe something then it must be true? (Of course, it might be true, but if the reason for believing it to be true is because most other people believe it to be true, this is an unsatisfactory justification, see **bad reasons fallacy**.)

It is important not to confuse this attack on the belief in truth by consensus or truth by majority opinion with an attack on democratic decision-making. The reason why democratic decision procedures are often preferable to other alternatives is not that they reliably give true answers to questions, but that they allow for equal participation of different interest groups and usually provide ways of minimising the power of would-be tyrants (but see **democratic fallacy**).

tu quoque

Latin phrase meaning 'you too'. A variety of the **companions in guilt move**, the equivalent of saying 'this criticism doesn't just apply to my position; it applies to yours too.' (See also *ad hominem* **move** in the second sense given in that entry.)

U

universal expertise

Proficiency in one field taken as an indicator of proficiency in an unrelated one. Experts in one field often feel confident to comment on another area about which they know far less. Unwary members of the public may make the unreliable **assumption** that because someone is a recognised authority (see **truth by authority**) in a particular area he or she must be capable of speaking with equal authority on any other subject. But the assumption that anyone is an expert in every area is certainly false; the assumption that an expert in one area is an authority on unrelated areas is also usually false. The only reason for trusting experts is that they have expertise in the area on which they are pronouncing.

For instance, there is no doubt that Albert Einstein was a great physicist. We should take very seriously any pronouncements he made on physics, and indeed on related topics. But there is no reason to think that because he was a genius as a physicist his comments on the nature of society should be treated as authoritative. There is no obvious connection between the study of physics and the study of human society. Certainly he was a highly intelligent man; but the shortness of a human life means that many highly intelligent people are relatively poorly informed on a wide range of issues. This is most relevant when the area is one which requires detailed knowledge rather than the application of transferable thinking skills. It just isn't possible to be an expert on everything. (See also **kowtowing**.)

V

vagueness

Lack of precision. Vagueness should not be confused with **ambiguity**, which occurs when a word or phrase has two or more possible meanings. Vagueness is always relative to context: what is vague in one context might be precise in another.

For instance, when filling in your age on an application form for a passport it's no good writing 'over 18': that's far too vague. But, in a different context, such as when asked your age for the purposes of deciding whether or not you are eligible to vote in an election, saying 'over 18' may well be precise enough. When asked for directions to the Tower of London someone who replied, 'It's somewhere along the north bank of the Thames' would have given a very vague answer. It's not ambiguous, it just doesn't give precise enough information about how to get there. When answering questions in a general knowledge quiz, 'on the north bank of the Thames' may count as an accurate response.

Vagueness is an obstacle to efficient communication. Sometimes people who want to avoid committing themselves to a particular course of action use vagueness as a ploy. For instance, a politician asked how precisely he intends to save money in the public sector might make vague generalisations about the need for improved efficiency, which, while true, don't commit him to any particular way of achieving this. A good journalist would then press for further information about precisely how this efficiency was to be achieved, forcing him to come out from behind this veil of vagueness. Or someone who was late for an appointment but didn't want to admit that this was because he'd stopped for a drink on the way might say 'Sorry I'm late, I had something I needed to do on the way here and it took slightly longer than I expected', deliberately leaving the cause of the delay vague, and exercising a particular kind of **economy with the truth**.

validity

The truth-preserving quality of good deductive arguments (see **deduction**). Valid arguments guarantee true **conclusions** provided that their **premises** are true. Valid arguments with one or more false premises, however, will not guarantee true conclusions: they may have true conclusions, but you can't be sure of this simply on the basis of their validity. Validity should not be confused with truth. Validity is always a quality of the structure of arguments; statements are true or false. Arguments can never be true or false, statements never valid or invalid (except when using the words 'valid' and 'invalid' in a colloquial sense in which they are synonymous with 'true' and 'false', as in the sentence 'The prime minister's statement that taxes are far too high is valid'). Only deductive arguments can be valid or invalid.

For instance, consider the following argument:

If the fire alarm rings everyone should walk to the nearest exit.
The fire alarm is ringing.
So everyone should walk to the nearest exit.

The form of this argument is:

If *p* then *q*
p
Therefore *q*

The letters *p* and *q* are standing in for any cases that you might want to insert into the argument. Whatever cases you do insert will not affect the validity of the argument: as long as your premises are true, the conclusion must be true. Another example of exactly the same form of argument, a form which is known as **affirming the antecedent** (also known by its Latin name *modus ponens*) is:

> If anyone is caught breaking the law then they will be prosecuted.
> You have been caught breaking the law.
> So you will be prosecuted.

Again, if the premises are true, the truth of the conclusion is guaranteed.

The following is an invalid form of argument:

> All men are mortal.
> Fred is mortal.
> So Fred is a man.

This bears a superficial similarity to the valid argument form:

> All men are mortal
> Fred is a man
> So Fred is mortal

However, the difference is that the first example does not guarantee the truth of the conclusion that Fred is a man: the premises could both be true and yet Fred be a cat. Whereas in the second argument if we know that it is true that all men are mortal and that Fred is a man we can confidently state that it is true that Fred is mortal. Another name for an invalid form of argument is a **formal fallacy** (although the word 'fallacy' is also used in a looser sense to refer to any bad way of arguing, or even for a false belief; see **informal fallacy** and **'that's a fallacy'**).

Van Gogh fallacy

An unreliable form of **argument** which takes its name from the following case:

> Van Gogh was poor and misunderstood in his lifetime, yet he is now recognised as a great artist; I am poor and misunderstood, so I too will eventually be recognised as a great artist.

Although obviously **invalid**, this type of reasoning can be particularly seductive to struggling artists and is a disturbingly widespread form of **wishful thinking**. Usually the argument is not stated explicitly; rather it is implicit in the way people live. The same form of argument occurs in other contexts: e.g. 'Mick Jagger and I went to the same primary school; Mick Jagger turned out to be a great success, so I will do so too.'

What's wrong with the Van Gogh fallacy is that the class of poor, misunderstood and unrecognised people is much larger than the class of great artists or rock stars. Sharing some relatively common attribute with someone great in no way guarantees my greatness. It is only if that attribute is a cause of their being great, or has a one-to-one correlation (see **correlation = cause confusion**) with it that it is relevant at all; and even then it may be the sort of cause which only very rarely results in greatness. All that we can legitimately conclude from the premises of the argument is that being poor and misunderstood (or going to a particular primary school) does not rule out the possibility of greatness.

It is easy to demonstrate the foolishness of relying on the Van Gogh fallacy by means of parody: 'Beethoven had a heart and a spine and was a great composer; I have a heart and a spine, so I'll probably turn out to be a great composer.' In this form it is clear that the Van Gogh fallacy typically relies on a weak **analogy**: just because I resemble a great person in some unimportant respects, it does not follow that I resemble him in others.

vested interest

Having a personal investment in the outcome of a discussion: standing to gain if a particular **conclusion** is reached. People who have vested interests in particular outcomes often distort evidence or are economical with the truth (see **economy with the truth**) in order to achieve their desired end.

For instance, a mortgage adviser might have a vested interest in persuading a house buyer to take out a certain type of mortgage because she stands to make a substantial commission from this transaction. This might lead her to stress the merits of this over other types of mortgage. In this case, the danger is that the naïve house buyer might believe that he is getting impartial advice. The mortgage adviser may not resort to **lying**; she need only be economical with the truth to dupe the gullible customer.

Or, consider another example. A public librarian with a personal interest in vegetable gardening might have a vested interest in enlarging the vegetable gardening section of the library; this vested interest might blind him to the fact that very few of the readers, whom it is his role to serve, share his fascination for the topic. Knowing this fact about the librarian might change your attitude to the ever-expanding library section on vegetable gardening.

However, as simply pointing out that someone has vested interests in a particular outcome is an *ad hominem* **move** of the **getting personal** kind, it in no way demonstrates that they are less than impartial. Their arguments need to be examined, and the evidence they give assessed. Nevertheless, the discovery of vested interests should alert you to the possibility of bias in the way that reasons and evidence are put across, and the strong motives for such bias.

vicious circles

See **circular arguments** and **circular definitions**.

W

weak analogies

See **analogy, arguments from**.

weasel words

Words that seem to promise more than they deliver. Weasels can allegedly suck out the contents of an egg without breaking its shell; analogously those who use weasel words suck the meaning out of a sentence while apparently leaving it intact. This term is not particularly precise. Its most obvious use is in advertising.

For example, advertisers who declare the food they are selling to be a 'healthier alternative' need to specify precisely what the food is healthier than and why. If they cannot do this, then the weasel words 'healthier alternative' are meaningless – mere **rhetoric**.

wedge, thin end of

See **slippery slope argument**.

wishful thinking

Believing that because it would be nice if something were true, then it must actually be true. This pattern of thought is extremely common, and very tempting because it allows us to avoid unpalatable truths. In extreme forms it is a kind of self-deception; in milder forms, an unwarranted optimism. It is surprising the lengths to which some people will go and the **rationalisations** they will make in order to avoid confronting evidence that would undermine their wishful thinking.

For instance, someone who drinks ten pints of beer a day might persuade himself that it has no effect whatsoever on his health. This is very likely wishful thinking, since this amount of alcohol is significantly above medically approved levels of consumption. In order to maintain the belief that the drink has no effect on his health, the drinker would probably have to ignore various symptoms or attribute them to other causes. When he drives home from the pub after drinking ten pints, he might believe that his driving is unimpaired by the alcohol because it's more convenient for him to drive than to take a taxi. Again, this would be an example of wishful thinking, since his reaction times, co-ordination and judgement would certainly be seriously affected by having this much alcohol in his system. His wishful thinking might actually be aided by the affects of alcohol, his logical processes being befuddled by the drink so that he does not see the possible con-sequences of his actions and so mistakenly believes that drink-driving laws need not apply to him. As this last example shows, wishful thinking can be dangerous since it puts a veil between us and the truth.